MW01679737

PROPER SPREADSHEET DESIGN

Maureen C. Thommes

bf

BOYD & FRASER PUBLISHING COMPANY
Boston

CREDITS:

Acquisitions Editor: James H. Edwards
Production Coordinator: Pat Stephan
Marketing Manager: Christopher Will
Manufacturing Director: Dean Sherman
Cover Design: Dick Hannus
Cover Photo: Superstock, Inc.
Composition: Beckwith-Clark, Inc.

© 1992 by boyd & fraser publishing company
A Division of South-Western Publishing Company
Boston, MA 02116

All rights reserved. No part of this work may be reproduced or used in any form or by any means—graphic, electronic, or mechanical, including photocopying, recording, taping, or information and retrieval system—without written permission from the publisher.

Manufactured in the United States of America

Library of Congress Cataloging-in-Publication Data
Thommes, Maureen C.
Proper spreadsheet design / Maureen C. Thommes.
p. cm.
Includes index.
ISBN 0-87835-850-1
1. Electronic spreadsheets. 2. Business—Computer programs.
HF5548.2.T4445 1992
650'.0285'536—dc20 91-30458
CIP

1 2 3 4 5 6 7 8 9 M 4 3 2 1

Dedicated with love and appreciation
to all my former teachers

CONTENTS

PREFACE

ABOUT THIS BOOK

Proper Spreadsheet Design addresses a strong interest of the academic community and the business world in a book that focuses solely on the design, documentation, and testing aspects of spreadsheet usage.

This book is designed for the beginning or intermediate user of spreadsheet software. **Proper Spreadsheet Design** is intended to be used with any spreadsheet program and in conjunction with a spreadsheet tutorial, reference manual, or textbook. Though the examples and suggested commands are presented in Lotus 1-2-3, transferring to other spreadsheet packages such as Quattro Pro or SuperCalc is easy because the examples deal with issues that are not software specific.

Proper Spreadsheet Design takes the user through the various phases of the planning and design, layout, testing, documentation, and auditing of spreadsheet applications. Numerous examples are presented to illustrate variations in problem type and approach. Each chapter contains a set of layout and design exercises that is suitable for use in the classroom or in employee training sessions.

ANCILLARY MATERIALS

An instructor's manual featuring suggestions for integrating the spreadsheet design concepts into an introductory course, workshop and employee training strategies, solutions to exercises in the text, and a data disk containing the Lotus 1-2-3 version of all spreadsheets used in the text, is available from the publisher.

ACKNOWLEDGMENTS

The author wishes to thank the following reviewers, whose comments help make this textbook stronger:

James Broslma	Kimberly Clark Corporation
James Bovinet	Winona State University
Carl Clavadetscher	California State Polytechnic University—Pomona
Richard Perrault	Chippewa National Forest
Wayne Vrioni	Cargill, Inc.
Lorraine M. Wittner	Minnesota State Department of Transportation

Special thanks also to Geoffrey Caufman for his sharing of ideas and strategies implemented at Cargill, Inc., and my fellow faculty members in the Business Administration and Accounting departments.

In addition, I wish to thank the dedicated professionals at Boyd and Fraser Publishing Company, especially Thomas K. Walker, James H. Edwards, Rosanne Coit, and Pat Stephan for their good ideas, hard work, and invaluable support.

Chapter 1 CRITERIA FOR GOOD SPREADSHEET DESIGN

INTRODUCTION

Since its invention in 1979, spreadsheet software has proven to be one of the most useful and popular of all the productivity software products. It is now commonly recognized that the introduction of the spreadsheet program was the most important contributing factor in the dramatically increased sale of microcomputers to the public and the world of end users. The competition among software industry leaders in the spreadsheet market is intense. Improvement, innovation, and evolution of spreadsheet software and spreadsheet tools continue to provide end users with increasingly sophisticated ways to organize, analyze, and present information.

One of the particularly useful aspects of spreadsheet software is its ability to provide a creative, flexible tool for users of various skill levels who are then able to create anything from the simplest worksheet to the most complex application with relative ease. The worksheet structure and the simple menu interface provide a framework useful for the solution of a wide variety of problems and applications.

Users of spreadsheets range from those with little formal training in data processing to the more experienced professional. As spreadsheets become widely used as an essential tool of the work world, certain conventions and standards have developed. These conventions and standards allow the user of spreadsheets greater ease in understanding, using, and changing their applications.

Yet, any attempt to establish or encourage particular conventions and standards for spreadsheets should be balanced by the recognition that spreadsheets are an extremely versatile and flexible tool that can be creatively utilized for a wide variety of problem solution strategies. It should be emphasized that design guidelines, controls, or conventions are best applied only to applications that clearly benefit from these strategies. Some problems have a methodology and format unique to the particular problem type. Some examples would include certain statistical and mathematical techniques such as linear programming, queuing, and inventory analysis. Though these problems will also have clearly delineated inputs and outputs, a layout that follows the customary presentation of these models may be more suitable.

Design conventions and standards for spreadsheets are best applied and utilized when their benefits are clearly understood and when they are applied appropriately to the particular application. It is important for the spreadsheet user to develop an understanding of the criteria for good spreadsheet design before attempting to apply any of these standards or conventions.

ACCURACY

The first criterion of good spreadsheet design must be accuracy. If the spreadsheet provides incorrect results, it clearly is of no value. Spreadsheets can be more susceptible to undetected errors than the standard computer program. The formulas and functions of a worksheet are not immediately visible to the user. The worksheet itself has few built-in error detection/protection features. And, because many spreadsheet users are not highly trained in software testing, most application designs do not include customized error detection/protection devices.

Good design and documentation can make the spreadsheet application more understandable and less susceptible to incorrect use. Controls can be built into the template that reduce the possibility of data error. Cross-checking, batch totals, and the breakdown of lengthy formulas into smaller steps are some of the error-reducing features users can build into spreadsheet templates. Careful, complete testing can detect any errors or verify all calculated results. In some situations, the spreadsheet application will be subjected to an internal audit. Ensuring that the template functions accurately will be one of the major requirements of the audit.

CLARITY

Spreadsheets need to be understood by both their creators and, in many situations, other users of the template or model. Clear, complete documentation and a standardized, consistent approach to layout design contribute much toward comprehensibility.

Spreadsheet documentation should include both direct documentation within the worksheet and supporting documentation that includes cell-formula listings, test data sets with correct test results, and an overall explanation of the application.

FLEXIBILITY

Spreadsheets need to be easily adapted to the changing aspects of a problem or application. If the initial design makes change and adaptation difficult or time-consuming, users will not derive full value from their initial work. Good design can contribute greatly toward creating a productive spreadsheet application. In the initial planning, consideration should be given to possible future uses or variations of the proposed model. Accommodation to these possibilities is recommended.

EFFICIENCY

Spreadsheets need to be efficient in at least two ways. Good design can ensure that the worksheet will require a minimum amount of memory for operation and processing. And, more importantly, good design can also ensure that the user will be able to readily locate and observe the critical portions of the worksheet. Thus, both human and machine will be as efficient as possible. The use of a design strategy in and of itself can help spreadsheet developers work more efficiently. The benefits of using a tested methodology has been demonstrated in several different areas and disciplines. Because spreadsheet software is relatively new and usage can be so flexible, spreadsheet design methodology has received little attention. As spreadsheets become increasingly vital to the work world, attention to efficient methodologies will grow.

AUDITABLE

A spreadsheet application may often be used only as an individual support tool for planning and decision-making. But, increasingly, spreadsheets are used to handle basic business functions. Accounting, inventory, and payroll applications are often implemented with spreadsheet systems. In these cases, the application will need to be audited as part of the general business audit. In such applications, a documented transaction trail may be required. Minimally, any calculated result should be traceable to the input values and operations that produced that result. The spreadsheet application should be designed to enable all required audits to be easily performed.

Spreadsheet applications may also be required to meet specific internal, operational controls that have been established by the business or organization. These controls may include specific guidelines regarding documentation and testing of the initial template and template modifications. Internal controls may also specify procedures for security and access controls for the template and for data files.

All of these criteria may be achieved using techniques and strategies contained in standard approaches to spreadsheet design, which are presented in the following chapters.

LAYOUT AND DESIGN EXERCISES

1. Critique a spreadsheet template or application that you have been currently using. (Use the criteria specified in Chapter 1.) Would you have changed your design in any way to better support the design criteria presented here?

2. Critique a current spreadsheet template or application for the clarity of its audit trail. Can you describe exactly what was done with the input data to achieve the output?
3. Should responsible businesses require that all spreadsheets used within the firm be audited or certified? What are the consequences of either doing or not doing this, in terms of both personnel and fiscal implications?

Chapter 2 PROPER LAYOUT AND DOCUMENTATION

The design paradigm most applicable to spreadsheets is the basic data processing model of INPUT–PROCESSING–OUTPUT. This model is utilized in the analysis and design of any type of computer-based application. It can be utilized as effectively in the analysis and design of computer programs and systems as in the analysis and design of spreadsheet templates and applications. In addition, when the user engages in a design strategy or process, that analytical activity can be extremely helpful in creating appropriate structure for an unstructured problem.

DESIGN APPROACH

The most effective design "tool" at this stage of thinking and planning is paper and pencil. A rough sketch of the basic regions of a proposed application that shows the general regions and basic contents of the worksheet provides a very useful overall plan. Sometimes, using technical tools for overall planning leads to premature focus on details. The user focuses too quickly on the contents of the cell instead of the structure of the problem. An overview of the major components and their relationships is an essential phase of planning and design. The effective use of the INPUT–PROCESSING–OUTPUT paradigm provides a simple strategy and appropriate guide in the creation of this master plan.

The application of the INPUT–PROCESSING–OUTPUT paradigm to spreadsheet design will require the following problem analysis activities. First, the user will need to identify the input and output data used in the problem. Input data can be defined as the raw data that describes the situation or problem being modeled. In a monthly budgeting model, for example (Figure 2-1), the input data will be the current monthly income and expenses.

A	A	B	C	D
1	MONTHLY BUDGET		INPUT DATA	
2				
3	EXPECTED CHANGE RATE -		1.5%	
4				
5			CURRENT MONTH	
6	INCOME:			
7	Wages		$1,500	
8				
9	EXPENSES:			
10	Rent		$400	
11	Car Payment		$150	
12	Utilities		$75	
13	Household		$350	
14	Miscellaneous		$200	
15				

Figure 2-1 Monthly Budget—Input Data

Output data is the data that is the result of calculations or other processing applied to the input data. In the monthly budget example, the output data will be the projected increase (or decrease) in income and expenses for future months. This projection could be based on several possible change factors, including the estimated inflation rate or growth rates. The output data is designated with x's in Figure 2-2.

A	A	B	C	D	E	F
1	MONTHLY BUDGET		INPUT DATA		OUTPUT DATA	
2						
3	EXPECTED CHANGE RATE -		1.5%			
4						
5			CURRENT MONTH		NEXT MONTH	
6	INCOME:					
7	Wages		$1,500		xxxxx	
8						
9	EXPENSES:					
10	Rent		$400		xxx	
11	Car Payment		$150		xxx	
12	Utilities		$75		xxx	
13	Household		$350		xxx	
14	Miscellaneous		$200		xxx	
15						
16	NET PROFIT/LOSS		xxxx		xxxx	
17						

Figure 2-2 Monthly Budget—Input and Output Data

Next, the user will need to identify and describe all of the processing required to produce the desired output. Processing is defined as the calculating, sorting, or selection that is applied to the input data to generate the resulting output data. In the monthly budget example, the processing consists of applying some type of change factor to the income and expense data in order to calculate projected income and expense values for future months. In spreadsheets, processing can usually be described in terms of the formulas, functions, sorts, and data queries performed on the input data (Figure 2-3).

```
FORMULAS for the NEXT MONTH PROJECTION
(for all INCOME & EXPENSE values for the current MONTH)

NEXT MONTH's value = CURRENT MONTH's value * (1 + change rate)
NET PROFIT/LOSS = INCOME - (TOTAL of all Expenses)
```

Figure 2-3 Formulas for the Next Month Projection

After the user has identified and described the specific INPUT–PROCESSING–OUTPUT required by the problem or application, a suitable plan will be needed to specify the location of these components in the worksheet. The most basic rule in designating a layout plan for any worksheet is:

CLEARLY IDENTIFY AND SEPARATE
INPUT DATA FROM OUTPUT DATA!!

Whatever the layout strategy, this basic rule, distinguishing INPUT from OUTPUT, is most critical in ensuring accurate and understandable templates. Surprisingly, this rule is often the one most often compromised. From an auditing perspective, clear delineation of inputs and their processed results provides the basis for identification of an accurate audit trail.

An effective layout for the monthly budget model is presented in Figure 2-4.

This layout is convenient for handling the planned output—a printed report showing both input and output data.

```
A         A                  B        C       D        E        F        G        H        I        J
1    MONTHLY BUDGET AND PROJECTION          FORMULAS for the NEXT MONTH PROJECTION
2    Author: M. Thommes                     (for all INCOME & EXPENSE values for the current MONTH)
3    Date Created: 6-28-91
4    Date Last Modified: N/A                NEXT MONTH's value = CURRENT MONTH's value * (1 + change rate)
5                                           NET PROFIT/LOSS = INCOME - (TOTAL of all Expenses)
6    .............................................................................................
7    INPUT DATA                        |    OUTPUT DATA
8                                      |
9    Expected Change Rate     1.50%    |
10                                     |    NEXT MONTH - PROJECTED BUDGET
11   INCOME                            |
12                  Wages   $1,500     |      $1,523
13                                     |
14   EXPENSES:                         |
15                   Rent     $400     |        $406
16            Car Payment     $150     |        $152
17              Utilities      $75     |         $76
18              Household     $350     |        $355
19          Miscellaneous     $200     |        $203
20                                     |
21        NET PROFIT/LOSS     $325     |        $331
22                                     |
23                                     |
24
```

Figure 2-4 Monthly Budget Projection

LAYOUT STRATEGIES

Separating the spreadsheet into specific use areas has become a commonly used layout strategy. However, not all users agree on just where some of the areas should be located. Some of these differences are not very important and are simply based on personal preference. However, in some cases, different layout patterns have been developed to support particular problem types or applications.

BLOCKED LAYOUT

There are two major approaches to layout—blocked and linear. The blocked strategy is most often used for smaller problems and is popular with beginners. That strategy is shown in Figure 2-5.

```
IDENTIFICATION AREA DOCUMENTATION AREA     WORK AREA       MACRO MENUS
Author:             Definitions            Query Criteria    & MACROS
Date Created:       Assumptions            Lookup Tables
Description:        Input Variables        Graph Labels
                    Constants
                    Formulas
                    Range Tables
                    Graph Tables
                    Layout Map

-----------------------------------------------------------------------
INPUT AREA                                  OUTPUT AREA
```

Figure 2-5 Layout Chart—Blocked Approach

The blocked approach groups the worksheet areas in the upper left-hand corner of the spreadsheet. For small templates, this strategy is quite acceptable. Most parts of the worksheet are easily visible in whole or part on a single screen with the cursor at the Home (cell A1) position. The major drawback of this strategy is the difficulty of expanding any of the areas. Expansion can be achieved only by inserting rows or columns, or by moving cell contents. In either case, some adjustments to formulas and macros may be required.

LINEAR LAYOUT

The linear approach to spreadsheet layout is depicted in Figure 2-6.

CONTROL AREA	IDENTIFICATION AREA	DEFINITIONS ASSUMPTIONS FORMULAS	WORK AREA	OUTPUT AREA	MACRO MENUS & MACROS
input data	author	range tables	lookup tables	data & labels	
	title	graph tables	graph labels		
	version	layout map	print formats		
	date				
	description				

Figure 2-6 Layout Chart—Linear Approach

This layout is much more flexible than the blocked approach. The linear approach allows ease in expanding downward for any of the areas. Documentation areas and data areas can be easily enlarged. It is also easier to select column widths appropriate for a single use rather than having to put a mixture of different data types, lengths, and formats into the same column.

Many beginning designers of spreadsheets like to use a layout that fits as much as possible into the area of the worksheet that can be viewed on a single screen. With effective use of range names, it is not necessary to actually see every part of the worksheet on the screen while writing formulas and creating output. The determining force for selection of a layout strategy should be the needs of the problem or application, and good documentation.

Whether a blocked layout or linear approach is used, the spreadsheet application should contain a set of critical areas that serve a specific function within the model.

IDENTIFICATION AREA

Every spreadsheet should begin with an identification that can be either immediately viewed on the opening screen or accessed by a range name. Spreadsheets should generally be saved with the cursor in the Home (cell A1) position. Then, subsequent retrieval of that file will result in a screen display with cell A1 in the upper left-hand corner. The identification should include a descriptive title, the spreadsheet author's name, and the date the spreadsheet was created. If the spreadsheet is a modification of an earlier version, appropriate information should be provided regarding the current version and its earlier versions. Version numbers and dates, and possibly a description of the variation for each version, can be included here.

CONTROL AREA

For some applications,the control area will hold data items that will be entered by spreadsheet users. These data items might be used for a data query or sort application. Or, the input parameters for a budget projection or loan/mortgage amortization model can be located in the control area. For such applications, the amount of control data will be relatively small and can be entered via the keyboard. In other applications, a control area may not be required at all. Macros are generally used to control the data entry process itself. Macros can also be used to receive sort and selection parameters. Illustrations of macro techniques are provided in Chapter 7, Macro Design.

ASSUMPTIONS, DEFINITIONS, AND FORMULAS

This area of the worksheet will contain much of the internal documentation for the entire application. At a minimum, this section should contain a listing and definition of all constants and input variables used in the spreadsheet. Range name tables, graph tables, and a layout map will also be placed in this area. A layout map can be used to document the layout areas and locations for the application.

Efficiency and productivity are enhanced if spreadsheet models are designed to be as general as possible. To accomplish this, all possible constants and input variables should be identified to allow the fullest range of flexibility and choice. For example, if a specific rate, such as a sales tax rate, is assumed to be set at a current value of 6% and used as a constant embedded in a formula, it may need to be changed at some future date. This change will be much more time-consuming if the constant is embedded within several formulas throughout the worksheet. Locating constant values in the input area and treating them as a special type of input variable greatly expands the generality of the template.

The documentation provided in this section can be extremely useful to other users of the model and to the model designer when changes need to be made. Formulas and definitions need not be checked by referring to the output area. Most of the information about the application can be observed directly from the documentation found in this section.

WORK AREA

The work area of an application can be used in a variety of ways. For data queries, it can serve as the criteria area. For printing tasks, it can hold printing formats or form letters; for graphs, it can hold additional data labeling information. Overall, there is some danger that this area could become quite cluttered and unorganized. It will be useful for the designer to consider possible needs of the application and mark off certain regions within the work area for those specific uses. Such possible regions could include lookup tables, print formats, and query areas. When a template is modified, the work area will frequently require enlargements and additions. This possible need for expansion should be taken into account in allocating space and locating the work area in the spreadsheet.

OUTPUT AREA

Since all input data has been located in the input area of the worksheet, the output area will contain only calculated results and descriptive labels. Some input data may need to be repeated to enhance understanding and readability. If any input data is referenced, it will be best to do so only via cell references or range names. Chapter 5 focuses on design of output in more detail.

The output area, as well as the input area, is located in a region of the worksheet where it can be easily expanded.

MACRO MENUS AND MACROS

Spreadsheet applications can utilize macros to provide either overall control with customized menus, or ease of use for particular routine tasks. In any case, the macros used in the application should be located in a consistent, contiguous area of the worksheet. This strategy makes utilization and reference to these macros considerably easier. Appropriate macro use will be discussed in greater detail in Chapter 7, Macro Design.

A major reason for using any kind of layout strategy is the need to create an organized approach to how the worksheet is used. Organization, orderliness, and documentation are the critical needs. In the selection of a layout strategy, these concerns must be addressed effectively. A layout pattern should be treated as a tool that helps present the problem effectively and accurately. A tight, compact layout with little wasted space can reduce memory requirements and speed up processing. If the layout is organized and designed for easy expansion as well as for compactness, both flexibility and efficiency can be achieved.

LAYOUT AND DESIGN EXERCISES

1. Describe the benefits derived from identifying and separating input data and output data for an application being developed on a spreadsheet.
2. For the following spreadsheet applications listed below, select the layout approach—blocked or linear—most suitable for the problem:
   a. 1040 tax form
   b. customer addresses—mailing list
   c. course grading system—including several tests, project grades, and a final exam
   d. departmental budget model—all categories are consistent and little change is expected
   e. an accounts receivable database
   f. an inventory file
   g. a club membership list, with dues, committee memberships, entry date, and birthdays
3. Using paper and pencil, develop a rough layout sketch, clearly marking all necessary areas, for any of the applications listed in Exercise 2.

Chapter 3 LAYOUT EXAMPLES

As indicated earlier, spreadsheet layouts will vary somewhat to accommodate different problem types. Some applications will have a small amount of input data and a larger amount of output. Other problems will contain a large amount of input data and comparatively smaller amounts of output. For some applications, the desired output will be displayed in cells and printed in the same format. Other applications will utilize output that consists of subsets selected from the larger pool of data. Usually such output is presented in a special report format, such as a mailing label, form letter, client bill, or check. Templates will sometimes be designed to reflect a predefined reporting model such as a pro forma income statement. Other templates may be designed with data arranged in columnar fashion as in a database. With such a variety of problem types, it is important to be flexible in layout and at the same time apply consistent standards of control, documentation, and testing.

3-YEAR INCOME PROJECTION—SMALL INPUT, LARGE OUTPUT

The example shown in Figure 3-1 of a typical 3-year income projection illustrates a commonly used predefined report format. This design can be improved

A	A	B	C	D	E	F
1						
2			3-YEAR INCOME PROJECTION			
3						
4	Expected Annual Growth Rate	5%				
5	Cost of Goods Sold					
6	as Percentage of Sales	60%				
7						
8						
9		1990	1991	1992	1993	
10						
11	GROSS SALES	35,750	37,538	39,414	41,385	
12						
13	Employee Sales Commissions	715	751	788	828	
14						
15	NET SALES	35,035	36,787	38,626	40,557	
16						
17	Cost of Goods Sold	21,450	22,523	23,649	24,831	
18						
19	GROSS PROFIT	13,585	14,264	14,977	15,726	
20						
21	Tax	6,521	6,847	7,189	7,548	
22						
23	NET PROFIT	7,064	7,417	7,788	8,178	
24						
25						

Figure 3-1 3-year Income Projection—Initial Version

considerably by applying the design strategies and the blocked layout pattern presented in Chapter 2.

Some attempt to identify and separate the input data has been made by providing an area near the top of the worksheet for the annual growth rate and COGS percentage. However, not all of the input data has been successfully identified and located in this input region. The initial gross sales for the first year is a critical input data item.

In addition, the definitions and calculations used to derive sales commissions and taxes are not immediately evident. Though the definitions of gross sales, gross profit, and net sales are standard and evident to someone with an accounting background, these definitions may be useful clarifications for some potential users of this model.

The model could be generalized further by identifying the commission rate, the tax rate, the first-year gross sales, and the value of the first year.

This application has been redesigned and is presented in Figure 3-2.

In the version presented in Figure 3-2, the input variables have been expanded to include both the first-year gross sales and those of the current year. This generalized model can accommodate a greater range of input variables and thus serve a broader range of problems. Additional information about the model is also presented immediately to the user of the revised model. The commission rate and tax rate are immediately and clearly identified. And, the fiscal year labels can be adjusted and controlled from the input area.

Space is left in the upper right-hand area of the worksheet for a work area and for worksheet macros. For this worksheet, appropriate macros could be developed to control data entry for the input area and printing of the 3-year income projections in the output area. Macros could also be developed to present output data in graphical formats.

A	A	B	C	D	E	F	G	H	I
1									
2	3-YEAR INCOME PROJECTION			Assumptions, Definitions, Formulas:					
3	Author: M. Thommes								
4	Date Created: 6-8-91			Standard Commission Rate = 2%					
5	Date Last Modified: N/A			Standard Tax Rate = 48%					
6									
7	....			Net Sales = Gross Sales - Commissions					
8	WORK AREA			COGS = Gross Sales * COGS percentage					
9				Gross Profit = Net Sales - COGS					
10				Net Profit = Gross Profit - Tax					
11									
12				Input Variables:					
13				lst year Gross Sales - cell B25					
14				Expected Annual Growth Rate -cell B26					
15				COGS Percentage - cell B27					
16				Current Sales Year - cell B28					
17									
18									
19									
20									
21									
22									
23	....								
24	INPUT DATA			3-Year INCOME PROJECTION					
25	1st Year Gross Sales	45,000		28-Sep-91	1995	1996	1997	1998	
26	Expected Annual Growth Rate	5%							
27	COGS Percentage	60%		GROSS SALES	45,000	47,250	49,613	52,094	
28	Current Sales Year	1995		Employee Commissions	900	945	992	1,042	
29				NET SALES	44,100	46,305	48,621	51,052	
30	Employee Commission Rate -	2.00%		Cost of Goods Sold	27,000	28,350	29,768	31,256	
31	Tax Rate -	48%		GROSS PROFIT	17,100	17,955	18,853	19,796	
32				Tax	8,208	8,618	9,049	9,502	
33				NET PROFIT	8,892	9,337	9,804	10,294	
34									
35									

Figure 3-2 3-year Income Projection—Revised Version

CHECKBOOK REGISTER—A DATABASE EXAMPLE

A second layout example illustrates an application that has a large amount of input data arranged in columnar format as a database. The checkbook register shown in Figure 3-3 has been designed to illustrate several of the same features of good design

A	A	B	C	D	E	F	G	H
1			CHECK BOOK REGISTER					
2	Author: M. Thommes							
3	Date Created: 6-12-91							
4	Date Last Modified: N/A							
5								
6	....							
7								
8			CONTROL AREA					
9								
10								
11	Trans	Chk-no	Trans-date	Description	Amount	Code	Balance	
12						loan		
13								
14								
15								
16								
17								
18								
19								
20								
21								
22	....							
23	Past Balance =		550.00					
24								
25		CHECK BOOK REGISTER - 1991						
26								
27	Trans	Chk-no	Trans-date	Description	Amount	Code	Balance	
28	D		01-Jan-91	Payroll	3,000.00		3,550.00	
29	W	1001	03-Jan-91	Mortgage	950.00	mort	2,600.00	
30	W	1002	05-Jan-91	SS Credit Union	350.00	loan	2,250.00	
31	W	1003	08-Jan-91	VISA-boat pymt	200.00	loan	2,050.00	
32	W	1004	08-Jan-91	Northern Electr	55.90	util	1,994.10	
33	W	1005	12-Jan-91	Cub Foods	75.89	groc	1,918.21	
34	W	1006	15-Jan-91	Fred's Corner D	35.89	hlth	1,882.32	
35	W	1007	17-Jan-91	Sylvie's	102.90	clth	1,779.42	
36	D		17-Jan-91	Payroll	3,000.00		4,779.42	
37	W	1008	18-Jan-91	Ted's Barbersho	12.00	clth	4,767.42	
38	W	1009	25-Jan-91	Blue Moon	65.00	entrn	4,702.42	
39	W	1010	27-Jan-91	Theil's Hardwar	350.95	misc	4,351.47	
40	W	1011	28-Jan-91	Bentley College	780.00	misc	3,571.47	
41	W	1012	30-Jan-91	Quick Lube	35.00	car	3,536.47	
42	W	1013	30-Jan-91	Southern Bell	58.00	util	3,478.47	
43	W	1014	31-Jan-91	City Water	25.00	util	3,453.47	
44	W	1015	31-Jan-91	Dr. Pull	88.69	hlth	3,364.78	
45	W	1016	31-Jan-91	Blue Moon	109.00	entrn	3,255.78	
46								
47								
48								

Figure 3-3A
Checkbook Register

A	I	J	K	L	M	N
1			Assumptions,Definitions, Formulas			
2			Trans = withdrawal - W			
3				deposit - D		
4						
5			Exp-code = Expenditure Category			
6			groc	groceries,supplies		
7			util	electric,water,gas		
8			mort	house mortgage		
9			loan	installment loans-car,boat		
10			hlth	health care-doctor,dentist,drugs		
11			clth	clothing,hair care		
12			entrn	entertainment		
13			car	car expenses		
14			misc	other uncategorized expenses		
15						
16						
17						
18						
19						
20						
21						
22	....	....	....	....	....	....
23						
24			OUTPUT AREA			
25						
26						
27	Trans	Chk-n	Trans-date	Description	Amount	Code
28	W	1002	05-Jan-91	SS Credit Union	350.00	loan
29	W	1003	08-Jan-91	VISA-boat pymt	200.00	loan
30						
31						
32						
33						
34						
35						
36						
37						
38						
39						
40						
41						
42						
43						
44						
45						
46						
47						
48						

Figure 3-3B
Checkbook Register

shown in the previous example. A blocked layout strategy is again implemented.

In the checkbook register, the data area holds the entire set of data. In the example, the control area holds the criteria for a / Data Query Extract for the code value of "loan." The output area holds the results of the Extract command. The output area serves only as a region for holding reports or outputs. These outputs could be the results of a / Data Query Extract or another type of report, such as a monthly statement reconciliation.

PAYROLL—AN EXAMPLE WITH LOOKUP TABLES

The third example of a spreadsheet layout (Figure 3-4) illustrates the use of lookup tables that are located in the work area. Calculations performed in the output area reference data in table format through the @VLOOKUP function.

Two tables are located in the work area. The tables are each assigned a range name—MARRIED and SINGLE. These tables are used to look up the federal tax withholding for the corresponding number of exemptions, marital status, and gross pay. In this example, the data in the input area is again arranged in columnar format. The data in the output area is also arranged in columnar format, with rows of calculated data corresponding to the input rows. These tables can be easily referenced in formulas by using their range names after appropriate range names have been assigned using / Range Name Create (in Lotus).

A	A–E	F	G	H	I	J
1	PAYROLL SYSTEM		WORK AREA			
2	Author: M. Thommes					
3	Date Created: 6-14-91	MARRIED - Semimonthly payroll				
4	Date Last Modified: N/A	wages	allowances			
5			0	1	2	3
6	....	$500	$57	$45	$33	$21
7	Assumptions, Definitions, Formulas	$520	$60	$48	$36	$24
8		$540	$63	$51	$39	$27
9	Regular pay = Pay Rate X Hours Worked(<=40)	$560	$66	$54	$42	$30
10	Overtime Pay = Pay Rate X 1.5 X Overtime Hours(>40)	$580	$69	$57	$45	$33
11		$600	$72	$60	$48	$36
12	WITHOLDINGS:	$620	$75	$63	$51	$39
13	Social Security = 7.51% of Gross Income	$640	$78	$66	$54	$42
14	State Income Tax = 5% of Gross Income	$660	$81	$69	$57	$45
15		$680	$84	$72	$60	$48
16	Federal Income Tax - lookup on tax tables	$700	$87	$75	$63	$51
17		$720	$90	$78	$66	$54
18	FEDERAL TAX TABLES-based on marital status	$740	$93	$81	$69	$57
19	MARRIED F6..L21	$760	$96	$84	$72	$60
20	SINGLE N6..T21	$780	$99	$87	$75	$63
21		$800	$102	$90	$78	$66
22	INPUT VARIABLES:					
23	Employee Name					
24	Marital Status - S = Single, M = married					
25	Number of Exemptions					
26	Hourly Wage Rate					
27	Hours Worked - Regular or Overtime					
28						

29	....								
30		INPUT DATA							OUTPUT AREA
31	Employee	Marital	Number of	Regular	Overtime	Hourly	Regular	Overtime	Gross
32	Name	Status	Exemption	Hours	Hours	Wage	Pay	Pay	Pay
33	Earl Baker	S	0	80	0	$12.00	$960.00	$0.00	$960.00
34	Carl Jones	M	5	80	10	$15.00	$1,200.00	$225.00	$1,425.00
35	Jane Hamilton	S	1	75	0	$8.75	$656.25	$0.00	$656.25
36	Peter Smith	M	4	60	0	$12.50	$750.00	$0.00	$750.00
37	Angell Labourx	M	5	80	0	$8.90	$712.00	$0.00	$712.00
38	Esther Albertson	M	3	80	5	$6.25	$500.00	$46.88	$546.88
39	Carrie Walker	S	0	80	8	$13.00	$1,040.00	$156.00	$1,196.00
40	James Brown	M	3	55	0	$12.00	$660.00	$0.00	$660.00
41	Joan Caulfield	M	4	79	0	$8.50	$671.50	$0.00	$671.50
42									

Figure 3-4A Payroll

A	K	L	M	N	O	P	Q	R	S	T
1										
2										
3				SINGLE - Semimonthly payroll						
4				wages	allowances					
5	4	5			0	1	2	3	4	5
6	$9	$0		$500	$70	$58	$46	$33	$21	$9
7	$12	$0		$520	$73	$61	$49	$36	$24	$12
8	$15	$3		$540	$76	$64	$52	$39	$27	$15
9	$18	$6		$560	$79	$67	$55	$42	$30	$18
10	$21	$9		$580	$82	$70	$58	$45	$33	$21
11	$24	$12		$600	$85	$73	$61	$48	$36	$24
12	$27	$15		$620	$88	$76	$64	$51	$39	$27
13	$30	$18		$640	$91	$79	$67	$54	$42	$30
14	$33	$21		$660	$94	$82	$70	$57	$45	$33
15	$36	$24		$680	$97	$85	$73	$60	$48	$36
16	$39	$27		$700	$100	$88	$76	$63	$51	$39
17	$42	$30		$720	$103	$91	$79	$66	$54	$42
18	$45	$33		$740	$106	$94	$82	$69	$57	$45
19	$48	$36		$760	$109	$97	$85	$72	$60	$48
20	$51	$39		$780	$112	$100	$88	$75	$63	$51
21	$54	$42		$800	$118	$103	$91	$78	$66	$54
22										
23										
24										
25										
26										
27										
28										
29	....	....	....	....						
30										
31	Soc Sec	Federal	State	Net						
32	FICA	FIT	SIT	Pay						
33	$72.10	$118.00	$48.00	$721.90						
34	$107.02	$42.00	$71.25	$1,204.73						
35	$49.28	$79.00	$32.81	$495.16						
36	$56.33	$45.00	$37.50	$611.17						
37	$53.47	$27.00	$35.60	$595.93						
38	$41.07	$27.00	$27.34	$451.47						
39	$89.82	$118.00	$59.80	$928.38						
40	$49.57	$45.00	$33.00	$532.43						
41	$50.43	$33.00	$33.58	$554.49						
42										

Figure 3-4B Payroll

LINEAR LAYOUT EXAMPLE

The next example (Figure 3-5) presents a customer address application using the linear layout style. This example illustrates several new features. In the definition section, a layout map provides a tiny snapshot view of the entire worksheet. This map is named with a range name of LAYOUT. The user can easily use this reference tool by selecting the F5 function key and entering "LAYOUT" when the "go to address:" is requested.

```
LAYOUT MAP
A1......B1 C1..  D1..  I1..N1 AA1.....
|         | |     |     |     |         |
| control | | ID  | DEF |data | macros  |
|   area  | |     |     |     |         |
|         | |     |     |base | & menu  |
|  label  | |     |     |     |         |
|  format | |     |     |     |         |
---------------------------------------
```

Figure 3-5
Layout Map

Several other areas of this customer address application are also marked with range names. The DEFINITIONS, actual customer DATABASE, CONTROL area, MACROS area, and data fields in the control and label format area are range-named. (The actual names used are DEFINITIONS, DATABASE, CONTROL, and MACROS.) A range name table (Figure 3-6) is placed in the DEFINITIONS section as documentation of those ranges.

The entire customer address application is presented in Figure 3-7.

RANGE NAME TABLE	
CITY	B4
CONTACTDT	B7
DATABASE	I1..N19
DEFINITIONS	D1..D7
ID	C1..C8
INPUT	A1..A9
LAYOUT	D9..G17
LINE1	A13
LINE2	A14
LINE3	A15
MACROS	AA1..AG25
NAME	B2
STATE	B5
STREET	B3
ZIP	B6

Figure 3-6
Range Name Table

Notice that a control area is located in the upper left-hand corner of the worksheet. Below the data file is a label format to be used in printing mailing labels. The data fields in the control area will be used to receive and display specific data values for any or all of the fields of the database. These values can be used as data query criteria for selection of data subsets or as a means of defining sort order.

The customer address application could have been arranged using the block approach. The choice of layout may be of lesser consequence for some applications. One guide in helping the user make this choice may be the conveniences that one or the other method provides for the particular problem. The most important issue in spreadsheet layout is the need to be systematic and to clearly dedicate areas for specific use. Good documentation and use of a layout map can communicate the specific approach that was applied. However, in an environment where many users may work with the same application, it may be extremely useful for the business or organization to prescribe a standard layout style. In such

```
A    A                      B            C                          D              E        F         G          H
1    CONTROL AREA                        CUSTOMER DATABASE          DEFINITIONS:
2    NAME:                               Author: M. Thommes         NAME - first + Last name
3    STREET:                             Date Created: 7-6-91       STREET - street or P.O. Box
4    CITY:                               Date Last Modified: N/A    CITY - city
5    STATE:                                                         ZIP - 9-digit zip code
6    ZIP:                                                           STATE - 2-letter state abbrev
7    DATE LAST CONTACT:                                             DATE-LAST-CONTACT - date last order placed
8
9                                                                   LAYOUT MAP
10                                                                  A1......B1 C1..  D1..  I1..N1 AA1.....
11                                                                  |         | |    |     |    |          |
12   LABEL FORMAT                                                   |control  | | ID | DEF |data| macros   |
13   Line 1                                                         |  area   | |    |     |    |          |
14   Line 2                                                         |         | |    |     |base| & menu   |
15   Line 3                                                         | label   | |    |     |    |          |
16                                                                  | format  | |    |     |    |          |
17                                                                  --------------------------------------
18
19                                                                  RANGE NAME TABLE
20                                                                  CITY           B4
21                                                                  CONTACTDT      B7
22                                                                  DATABASE       I1..N19
23                                                                  DEFINITIONS    D1..D7
24                                                                  ID             C1..C8
25                                                                  INPUT          A1..A9
26                                                                  LAYOUT         D9..G17
27                                                                  LINE1          A13
28                                                                  LINE2          A14
29                                                                  LINE3          A15
30                                                                  MACROS         AA1..AG25
31                                                                  NAME           B2
32                                                                  STATE          B5
33                                                                  STREET         B3
34                                                                  ZIP            B6
35
36
```

Figure 3-7A Customer Address File

A	I	J	K	L	M	N	O
1	NAME	STREET	CITY	STATE	ZIP	DATE-LAST-CONTACT	
2	Scott Anderson	1220 Albert St.	Georgetown	WI	23908-0909	02-Jan-89	
3	James Balan	560 Irvine Ave.	Iowa City	IO	89093-0910	06-Mar-90	
4	Darrel Bandy	1300 America Ave N.W	St. Paul	MN	55455-0000	10-Dec-90	
5	Olaf M. Bly	509 Scott Ave.	Jamestown	SD	67890-5008	08-Jul-86	
6	Mary Cleary	350 Minnesota Ave.	Albert Lea	MN	89099-0000	18-Mar-87	
7	Jody Duff	Box 12	Pine Lane	ND	98867-0012	20-Jul-89	
8	Mike Field	456 Rustic Lane	Ely	MN	89009-0000	06-Apr-88	
9	Barb Fisher	564 Albert St.	Denver	CO	89345-0120	04-Apr-89	
10							
11							
12							
13							
14							
15							
16							
17							
18							
19							
20							
21							
22							
23							
24							
25							
26							
27							
28							
29							
30							
31							
32							
33							
34							
35							
36							

Figure 3-7B Customer Address File

a case, the linear approach is recommended since it is most flexible and easily applied to a variety of problem types.

LAYOUT AND DESIGN EXERCISES

1. Develop a template for a loan/mortgage amortization model. Identify the INPUT (or control) data, the FORMULAS, and the OUTPUT area clearly in the template. Also, provide an identification area that includes a descriptive title, author, and date created. The formula used to calculate the monthly loan/mortgage payment can utilize the Lotus @ PMT function and can be set as shown:

   @PMT(loan amount,rate/12,term*12)

   where

   loan amount = the total principal
   rate = the annual interest rate
   term = the total number of years of the loan

2. Develop a template for a class grading system. Assume that there will be four tests administered to the class and the final grade for each student will be the average of the four tests. Clearly indicate the INPUT data, the FORMULAS, and the OUTPUT area. Provide an identification area that includes a descriptive title, author, and date the template was created.
3. Modify the template created in Exercise 2 to accommodate five tests instead of four tests. How easily is this change made? What changes would you make in the initial design to allow easier adjustment of the number of tests used to calculate the final grade?
4. Redesign the layout of the payroll application (Figure 3-4) using the linear approach. Start by drawing a rough sketch on paper and then implementing it using your spreadsheet program. Now add a print format that can be used to print an employee paycheck. Which layout strategy is most suitable to this application?

Chapter 4 RANGE NAMES, CONTROLS, AND FORMULAS

There are several design techniques that contribute to the flexibility and usefulness of a template. One of the most important of these techniques is the utilization of generic formulas and functions. Generic formulas can be achieved by following two basic design rules.

Rule One: Identify all input data and place it in a specifically designated area of the worksheet. It is the input data that will most likely be changed as variations and different applications are developed from the original template. Locating this data in its own area makes changes to the template easier. Also, it will be easier to ensure that all outputs will be the results of references to input data.

Rule Two: Use range names whenever possible for formulas and macros. There are two important benefits derived from the use of range names. First, formulas and macros become much more understandable and readable. This practice makes it easier to identify and locate errors. Second, if the template needs to be modified with an insertion of rows or columns, the affected range names are automatically adjusted (in Lotus) to the new cell addresses. This feature is extremely useful and time saving. Unfortunately, the table of range names does need to be recreated, using the / Range Name Table command, to reestablish the new cell references in the table.

Many spreadsheet users create their first templates by only using cell references, and often get so accustomed to the cell reference approach that the use of range names seems quite awkward. However, a range name is simply another way to refer to a single cell or a contiguous rectangular area of cells.

The use of range names requires some planning and time in the initial development of a template. This practice, along with most of the other design techniques presented in this book, increases efficiency considerably after the user becomes familiar with the technique. There is still a place for the "quick & dirty" spreadsheet. Yet it's important that the "quick & dirty" method does not become the standard of operation. Invariably, the user will want to re-use that quickly designed model. Having to endure the task of recalling and redesigning a poorly designed template is sometimes the best cure for the "quick & dirty" method.

Not long ago, I developed a "quick & dirty" retirement planning model, just to get a rough idea of the possibilities. Several months later, I wanted to reconsider those possibilities and referred to that "quick & dirty" model. It took more time than expected, and the assumptions that were embedded in formulas and not well documented took me some time to recognize. Even that simple model would have benefited from a better approach to design and documentation.

Some examples illustrating the benefits of the use of range names are given below. The first example (Figure 4-1) is the monthly budget projection first referenced in Chapter 2.

```
A          A                B          C          D          E          F          G          H          I          J
1    MONTHLY BUDGET AND PROJECTION               FORMULAS for the NEXT MONTH PROJECTION
2    Author: M. Thommes                          (for all INCOME & EXPENSE values for the current MONTH)
3    Date Created: 6-28-91
4    Date Last Modified: N/A                     NEXT MONTH's value = CURRENT MONTH's value * (1 + change rate)
5                                                NET PROFIT/LOSS = INCOME - (TOTAL of all Expenses)
6                                       RANGE NAMES TABLE
7                                       CARPYT   B26..B26
8                                       CHGRATE  B19..B19
9                                       EXPENSES B25..B29
10                                      HOUSE    B28..B28
11                                      MISC     B29..B29
12                                      PROJEXP  D25..D29
13                                      RENT     B25..B25
14                                      UTIL     B27..B27
15                                      WAGES    B22..B22
16   ...........................................................................................
17   INPUT DATA                             |    OUTPUT DATA
18                                          |
19   Expected Change Rate        1.50%      |
20                                          |    NEXT MONTH - PROJECTED BUDGET
21   INCOME                                 |
22                  Wages      $1,500       |         $1,523
23                                          |
24   EXPENSES:                              |
25                   Rent        $400       |           $406
26            Car Payment        $150       |           $152
27              Utilities         $75       |            $76
28              Household        $350       |           $355
29          Miscellaneous        $200       |           $203
30                                          |
31        NET PROFIT/LOSS        $325       |           $331
32                                          |
33                                          |
```

Figure 4-1 Monthly Budget Projection with Range Names

In this version, a range name table is added to the internal documentation of the template. Assume that the user wishes to add the expense category, child care, to the expense section. This requires the insertion of an extra row to the template, as shown in Figure 4-2. Without the use of range names, several formulas would require a cell reference

adjustment. With the use of range names, only the additional new range name and formula pertaining to the new expense category needs to be entered.

```
A         A                 B          C          D          E          F          G          H          I          J
1   MONTHLY BUDGET AND PROJECTION                 FORMULAS for the NEXT MONTH PROJECTION
2   Author: M. Thommes                            (for all INCOME & EXPENSE values for the current MONTH)
3   Date Created: 6-28-91
4   Date Last Modified: N/A                       NEXT MONTH's value = CURRENT MONTH's value * (1 + change rate)
5                                                 NET PROFIT/LOSS = INCOME - (TOTAL of all Expenses)
6                                      RANGE NAMES TABLE
7                                      CARPYT    B27..B27
8                                      CHGRATE   B20..B20
9                                      CHILDCAREB28..B28
10                                     EXPENSES  B26..B31
11                                     HOUSE     B30..B30
12                                     MISC      B31..B31
13                                     PROJEXP   D26..D31
14                                     RENT      B26..B26
15                                     UTIL      B29..B29
16                                     WAGES     B23..B23
17  ..............................................................................................
18  INPUT DATA                              |         OUTPUT DATA
19                                          |
20  Expected Change Rate       1.50%        |
21                                          |         NEXT MONTH - PROJECTED BUDGET
22  INCOME                                  |
23                 Wages      $1,500        |              $1,523
24                                          |
25  EXPENSES:                               |
26                  Rent        $400        |                $406
27           Car Payment        $150        |                $152
28            Child Care         $80        |                 $81
29             Utilities         $75        |                 $76
30             Household        $350        |                $355
31         Miscellaneous        $200        |                $203
32                                          |
33      NET PROFIT/LOSS         $245        |                $250
34                                          |
35                                          |
36
```

Figure 4-2 Monthly Budget Projection with Additional Expense Category

RANGE NAME DOCUMENTATION

Along with formulas and definitions, range names should be documented within the worksheet. A simple range name table can be placed in the assumptions, definitions, formulas area. In some cases where a large number of range names are used, this table can be placed in a more remote area of the worksheet or incorporated into the external documentation of the template.

In Lotus, range name tables can be created using the / Range Name Table command. This command writes a list of the range names to a two-column area in the worksheet assigned by you. This range table updates automatically if range names are adjusted by modifications to the worksheet. In creating the range table, the user needs to be certain that the area assigned for the table is large enough to contain all of the table information.

RANGE NAME DO'S AND DON'TS

1. *Do* use meaningful names for ranges up to 15 characters. *Do* use letters, digits, and either . or - as word connectors. *Do not* use spaces or punctuation symbols in range names.
2. *Do not* use cell addresses such as AA100 or B2 as a range name.
3. *Do* use range names to identify special regions of the worksheet:
   - a range of cells to be printed
   - a single cell or range of cells that is addressed in a macro

- a cell or range of cells used in a formula

  (The only time a range name CANNOT be used in a formula is in a calculation that reoccurs along a row or column.)

4. *Do not* use the / Range Name Reset command unless you really want to wipe out all of your current range names.

DATA CONTROLS

The most dangerous feature of spreadsheets is the possibility of having an undetected error in a worksheet. There have been several incidents in which very bad management decisions were made using erroneous data in a spreadsheet. Only good design and careful testing can reduce the possibility of such error. User-designed controls are absolutely necessary for any spreadsheet application, especially those containing financial data.

DATA CONTROL—GLOBAL PROTECTION

A simple control technique is the use of the PROTECT feature, which prevents users from changing the contents of a cell. This technique should be a standard requirement for any application used by more than one person. Once the template has been fully tested and is ready for operation, the designer can enable the global protection feature. In Lotus, the command series is / Worksheet Global Protect Enable. Those cells that will be open for data entry will then need to be unprotected using / Range Unprotect.

DATA CONTROL—VERIFICATION AND BATCH TOTALS

Professional programmers have several techniques at their disposal for data edit checks and data verification. Some of these techniques are easily applied to testing data accuracy within spreadsheets. Hash totals, batch totals, and cross-checked column totals are three such techniques. A batch total is used with a set of values that are grouped in a batch and that define specific data values such as currency or quantities. In contrast, a hash total is generally applied to a set of numbers whose total has no particular meaning. Identification numbers such as invoice numbers, social security numbers, and other identifications are often totaled in one stage of processing and compared to the total of the same group derived at another stage of processing, to ensure that the data set has not been altered in any way.

In the following sales commission example, all three of these techniques have been applied. Figure 4-3 shows the sales commission example with data values displayed.

Figure 4-4 shows the cells containing formulas formatted in text mode.

A hash total is used to sum the ID numbers of the salespersons receiving commissions. This hash total will then be compared to the hash total for ID numbers from previous and future sales commission reports. If all data sets and their IDs are unchanged, the hash totals should be identical. These techniques can be used to verify that the data sets have not been altered.

A	A	B	C	D	E	F	G
1		SALES COMMISSIONS					
2							
3	SALESPERSON	ID-Number	QTR1	QTR2	QTR3	QTR4	TOTAL
4							
5	M. James	234668900	$4,567.89	$4,567.90	$3,489.50	$2,356.56	$14,981.85
6	P. Smith	234658900	$2,345.00	$2,689.90	$3,490.80	$2,345.00	$10,870.70
7	J. White	348908977	$3,456.55	$5,634.00	$4,789.44	$2,545.78	$16,425.77
8	A. Alberts	365789002	$3,455.60	$2,390.84	$3,450.99	$2,900.90	$12,198.33
9	F. Schmidt	456335432	$2,800.78	$2,109.01	$2,230.88	$4,589.90	$11,730.57
10	G. Brew	489703345	$3,455.90	$3,674.90	$2,700.80	$2,509.04	$12,340.64
11	S. Jones	456229087	$2,389.78	$2,702.09	$2,101.23	$2,821.45	$10,014.55
12							
13	HASH TOTAL	2586293643					$88,562.41
14							
15	QUARTER TOTALS		$22,471.50	$23,768.64	$22,253.64	$20,068.63	$88,562.41
16							
17							
18							

Figure 4-3 Controls and Hash Totals

A batch total is used in several instances in the sales commissions report. Totals for each salesperson and each quarter, as well as a grand total, are generated. Again, these totals can be checked against other data to ensure accuracy.

Cross-checking is also applied in this example. The first grand total of annual commissions is generated by adding the totals for each quarter. The second grand total of annual commissions is generated as the sum of all salespersons' annual commissions. The two grand totals must be equal for this test to be successful.

These simple tests are standard and are typically required in applications that are audited. They do not ensure the accuracy of the data itself, but the tests can verify that the spreadsheet is working correctly.

A	A	B	C	D	E	F	G
1		SALES COMMISSIONS					
2							
3	SALESPERSON ID		QTR1	QTR2	QTR3	QTR4	TOTAL
4							
5	M. James	234668900	$4,567.89	$4,567.90	$3,489.50	$2,356.56	@SUM(C5..F5)
6	P. Smith	234658900	$2,345.00	$2,689.90	$3,490.80	$2,345.00	@SUM(C6..F6)
7	J. White	348908977	$3,456.55	$5,634.00	$4,789.44	$2,545.78	@SUM(C7..F7)
8	A. Alberts	365789002	$3,455.60	$2,390.84	$3,450.99	$2,900.90	@SUM(C8..F8)
9	F. Schmidt	456335432	$2,800.78	$2,109.01	$2,230.88	$4,589.90	@SUM(C9..F9)
10	G. Brew	489703345	$3,455.90	$3,674.90	$2,700.80	$2,509.04	@SUM(C10..F10)
11	S. Jones	456229087	$2,389.78	$2,702.09	$2,101.23	$2,821.45	@SUM(C11..F11)
12							
13	HASH TOTAL	@SUM(B5..B11)					@SUM(G5..G11)
14							
15	QUARTER TOTALS		@SUM(C5..C11)	@SUM(D5..D11)	@SUM(E5..E11)	@SUM(F5..F11)	@SUM(C15..F15)
16							
17							
18							

Figure 4-4 Controls and Hash Totals with Formulas

In some applications, additional controls may be applied to macro-controlled data entry routines. Several tests can be performed on the data by the macro. Values outside of acceptable ranges can be rejected. Coded values can be tested against a valid code table. Even check digits can be added to IDs, invoice numbers, order numbers, or other key fields.

It is actually quite difficult, and not always cost-effective, to build an application that is absolutely error-free. The cost in time, energy, and programming of implementing any controls must be weighed against the benefits afforded by the more accurate system or the losses incurred by possible errors. The perfect, error-free application is difficult to achieve and maintain. A certain healthy skepticism and constant review should accompany the use of any computer-based application.

FORMULAS

A good deal of time will be spent planning an application before the formulas are entered into their respective cells. Generally, range names should be defined before they are used in formulas. However, if a range name is defined for an area after this area has been referenced in a formula, Lotus will substitute that range name automatically in the formula.

When designing the application, lengthy formulas should be avoided. Instead, the long formula should be broken down into several stages that are placed in a series of cells. This strategy makes testing and error location considerably easier. Any later modifications to the formula or computational procedure are also much easier to apply.

Proper use of the @ROUND function will also prevent data errors due to incorrect rounding of the calculated results. In Lotus, the round-off function @ROUND(value,places) can be used to control the degree of accuracy needed for any data value or formula. Generally, use the @ROUND function wherever a specific degree of accuracy is required. Formulas requiring any arithmetic calculation with multiplication, division, addition, or subtraction should contain a @ROUND control.

LAYOUT AND DESIGN EXERCISES

1. Evaluate the sales commission example (Figure 4-4, with formulas) and select appropriate regions that should be assigned range names. Rewrite the formulas using those range names and create a range name table to document your ranges.

2. Using the sales commission application that you just developed in Exercise 1, add an IDENTIFICATION area, a DEFINITIONS area, and a LAYOUT map. Mark each of these with a range name so that you can easily reference these using the "go to address:" command—function key F5. Update your range name table.
3. Develop a set of controls appropriate for the payroll example, Figure 3-4 (pages 26–27). Since payroll is an application subject to audit, indicate how the controls you designed would be implemented.

Chapter 5 OUTPUT DESIGN

The presentation of the output, or results, of a spreadsheet requires some consideration from the design perspective. According to our design strategy, the output will be placed in a designated area of the worksheet. Apart from the benefits of separating input from output, this separate output area is useful when dealing with the presentation of output results.

There are several ways that a spreadsheet application can present output. These strategies are listed as follows:

1. A specific range of cells can be printed as is, with appropriate labeling and formatting to enhance readability.
2. The output can be presented in a graphical form, utilizing the presentation graphics options available (pie, line, and bar charts).
3. An output format can be designed and placed somewhere in the worksheet and a macro can be utilized to move specific data to the correct areas of that format. The form is printed repeatedly, as is done with mailing labels or a form letter.

Each of the methods of presenting output will be illustrated with examples. The design guidelines particularly suitable for the implementation of each strategy will be included and illustrated with each example.

PRINTING AN AREA OF THE WORKSHEET

Printing an area of the worksheet is the easiest and simplest way to present output results. The user will only need to identify the area or range of cells to be printed and add options such as headers, footers, and printer controls.

The area to be printed should have data labeled clearly. Numeric data should be formatted appropriately. When selecting a formatting option, the global format should be used first, with range formats to override the global format where needed. The global format requires considerably less memory than extensive use of range formats. The user will need to review the output area and select the format option applicable to the most cells as the global format. Following that, the cells that require a different format can be formatted with range format. In addition, the printed output should be identified with a title and date, if they are not provided within the worksheet. Header and footer lines are useful for such identifying data.

Two of our previous examples, the monthly budget projection and the 3-year pro forma income projection, are applications for which the user will want to display or print a specific area of the worksheet. In contrast, some spreadsheet applications have sets of input data that are being held largely for storage or record-keeping purposes. In these examples, the output is usually a smaller subset of data extracted or derived from the input data.

An example of a suitable printed area is shown in Figure 5-1 for the monthly budget projection example. In this version, the spreadsheet is formatted globally as currency with zero decimal places. The expected change rate is formatted as a percentage with two decimal places using the range option. The header is used to add a title and date. Generally, headers and footers should be used as efficient tools for labeling and dating all reports. Within the spreadsheet, the repeat symbol \'¦ is used to add a vertical line. Whenever such line markers are drawn, the repeat symbol followed by the selected character such as \. or * or \- is an efficient way to insert such lines. The use of the repeat symbol \ will always fill the entire cell, whatever the cell width, and adjust as cell widths are increased or decreased.

MONTHLY BUDGET PROJECTION - 28-Sep-91

Expected Change Rate	1.50%	|	
		|	NEXT MONTH - PROJECTED BUDGET
INCOME		|	
Wages	$1,500	|	$1,523
		|	
EXPENSES:		|	
Rent	$400	|	$406
Car Payment	$150	|	$152
Utilities	$75	|	$76
Household	$350	|	$355
Miscellaneous	$200	|	$203
		|	
NET PROFIT/LOSS	$325	|	$331

Figure 5-1
Monthly Budget Projection—Printed Report

The output for the 3-year pro forma income projection is shown in Figure 5-2. Again, a global format with currency and zero decimal places is used. Range formats are used on the cells displaying data in percent form. The title and date of the report are contained within the worksheet, so no header or footer is used.

Report Date - 28-Sep-91

INPUT AREA		3-Year INCOME PROJECTION				
1st Year Gross Sales	45,000	28-Sep-91	1995	1996	1997	1998
Expected Annual Growth Rate	5%					
COGS Percentage	60%	GROSS SALES	45,000	47,250	49,613	52,094
Current Sales Year	1995	Employee Commissions	900	945	992	1,042
		NET SALES	44,100	46,305	48,621	51,052
Employee Commission Rate -	2.00%	Cost of Goods Sold	27,000	28,350	29,768	31,256
Tax Rate -	48%	GROSS PROFIT	17,100	17,955	18,853	19,796
		Tax	8,208	8,618	9,049	9,502
		NET PROFIT	8,892	9,337	9,804	10,294

Figure 5-2 3-year Income Projection—Printed Report

In each of these examples, the input data as well as the resulting output data is included in the printed report. Notice that the layout of the spreadsheet with the input area adjacent to the output area makes it easy to present the results in a single contiguous area. When data is not so conveniently arranged, users can hide the rows or columns of data that are not to be contained in the report. Initially, reports that are to be printed should be designed to meet the needs of the printed report.

GRAPHICAL OUTPUT

Presentation graphics is one of the most innovative and useful features of spreadsheet software. The ease with which impressive pie charts, bar charts, and line graphs can be developed using data stored in the worksheet is a true user delight.

The challenge to the user is to develop graphs that communicate in a meaningful and accurate way. Each of the graph types presents information in a different way and is suitable for a different type of data set. A pie chart is used to show data that represents the parts of a whole. For example, in the monthly budget projection, a pie chart could be used to display the amount spent in each expense category—expense items as part of the total monthly expense. If parts of the whole are to be shown for more than one item, such as expense categories for total expense for several months, a multiple-range vertical bar chart is most appropriate. Horizontal bar charts are suitable for portraying data sets that are to be compared against each other. Line graphs are best for larger sets of data that cannot fit into a reasonably sized bar chart. Multiple-line graphs are effective when two or more data sets are to be compared over time.

To be sure that the graph communicates effectively and accurately, all axes and lines or bars need to be clearly labeled. The graph itself should contain an informative title and information about the time frame or dates of graphed data. Color should be used to highlight or contrast and draw attention to the focal point or intended message of the graph. Any additional data needed to produce graphs can be placed in the work area of the spreadsheet. Such data can include codes for hatch patterns or exploded sections for pie charts, and data labels used to label points on a line graph.

An example of a pie chart for our monthly budget projection is shown in Figure 5-3. It should be noted that the procedure of defining ranges for graphs becomes conceptually easier when using range names to address areas of data. The X and A ranges for this pie chart are easily assigned by specifying "categories" for the X-range and "expenses" for the A-range instead of using cell addresses.

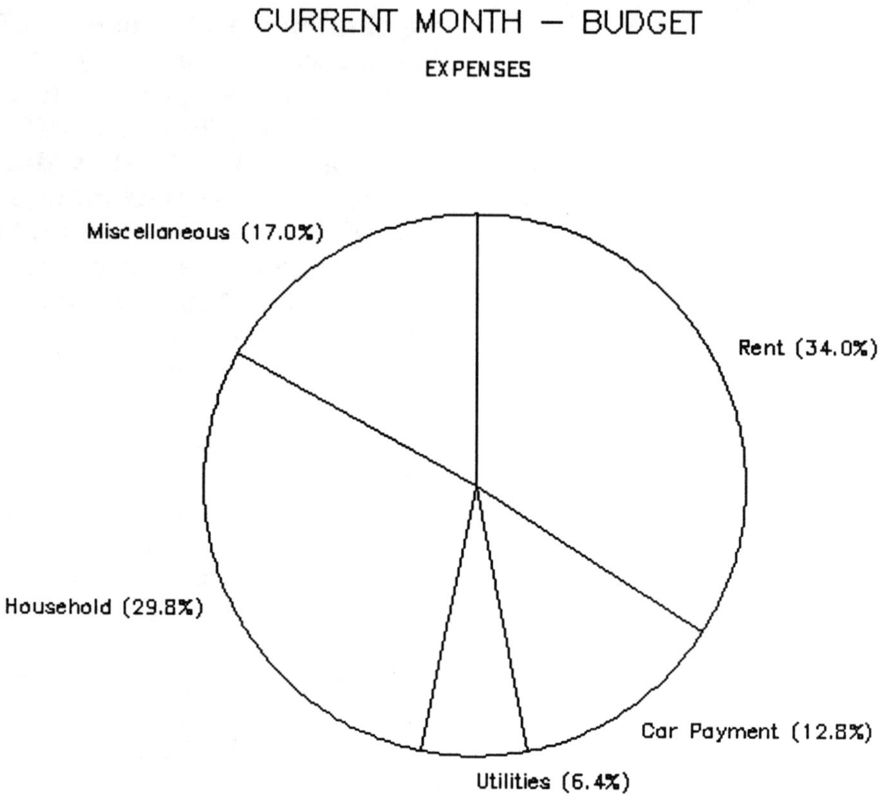

Figure 5-3 Monthly Expenses, Current Year—Pie Chart

A stacked-bar graph is used to show the various costs and net profits over a 3-year period for the pro forma income projection, as shown in Figure 5-4.

Graphs that have been developed for a particular application should be documented with the worksheet. A graphics table, similar to the range name table, can easily be created using the / Graph Name Table command series in Lotus. This graph table can be placed in the assumptions, definitions, formulas area, along with the range name table. As example of such a graph table is shown in Figure 5-5 for the 3-year income projection model.

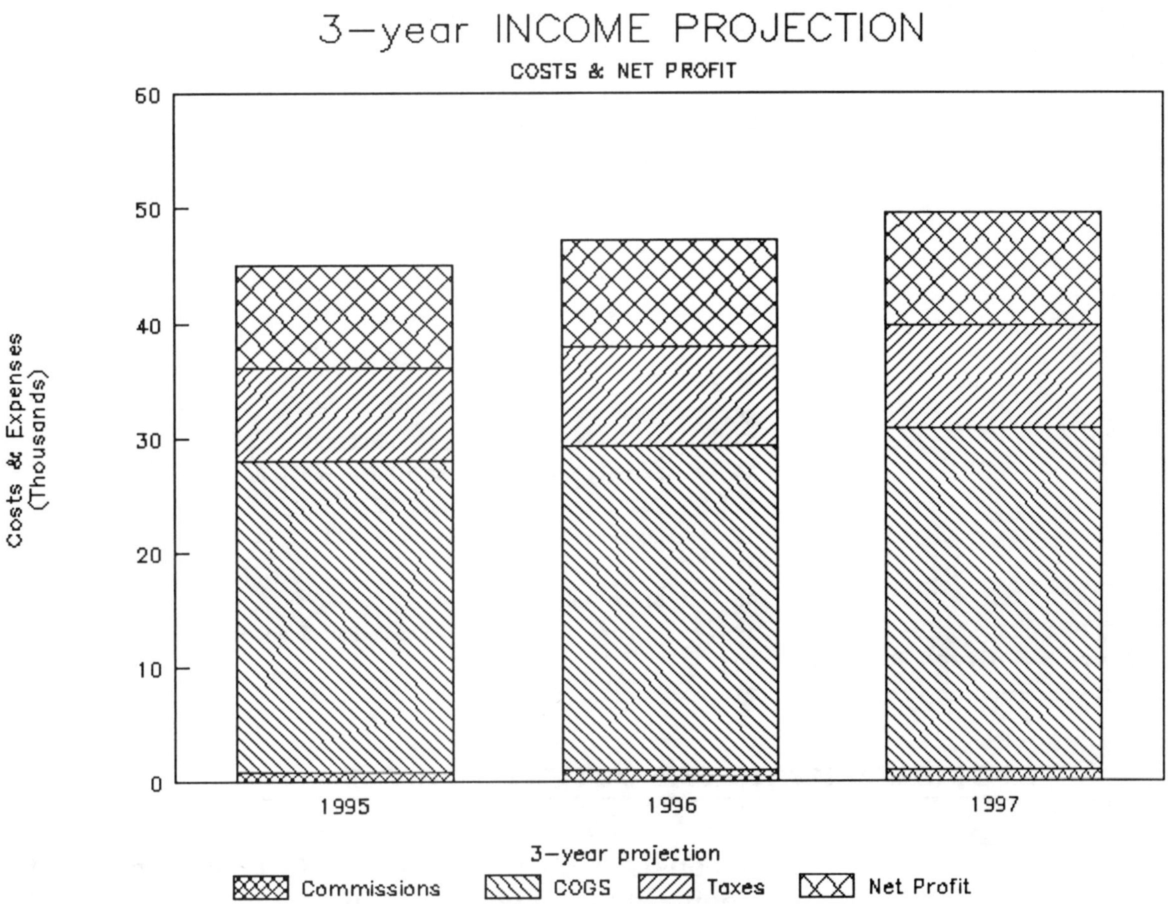

Figure 5-4 3-year Income Projection—Stacked-Bar Graph

A particular spreadsheet could also have an entire set of graphs designed to be accessed through a macro. Examples of this macro technique will be provided in Chapter 7, Macro Design.

```
A   C       D                   E         F           G           H
1
2      Assumptions, Definitions, Formulas:
3
4      Standard Commission Rate = 2%
5      Standard Tax Rate = 48%
6
7      Net Sales = Gross Sales - Commissions
8      COGS = Gross Sales * COGS percentage
9      Gross Profit = Net Sales - COGS
10     Net Profit = Gross Profit - Tax
11
12     Input Variables:
13     lst year Gross Sales - cell B25
14     Expected Annual Growth Rate -cell B26
15     COGS Percentage - cell B27
16     Current Sales Year - cell B28
17
18     Graph Table
19     FIG5-4              Stack-Bar 3-year INCOME PROJECTION
20
21
```

Figure 5-5 Graph Table for 3-year Income Projection

SPECIALLY DESIGNED OUTPUT FORMAT

A considerably more complex form of output is often required for some spreadsheet applications. Mailing labels, customized reports, form letters, and other such specially designed outputs can be developed with spreadsheets. Generally, these applications require a data-manipulation macro to move data from an input or output area to the appropriate locations on the customized form. The form itself will be located in the work area or the macro area of the spreadsheet. Examples of this output technique is provided in Chapter 7, Macro Design.

LAYOUT AND DESIGN EXERCISES

1. Refer to Figure 3-3, the checkbook register example (pages 23–24). Design several possible outputs for this application. Include simple printed reports, graphs, and specifically designed report formats.

   Hint: you will probably want to use some Data Query and Sort commands to select or re-order data.

Chapter 6 TESTING AND EXTERNAL DOCUMENTATION

The testing process is the final control applied to the spreadsheet development process. In a sense, testing is a type of user-conducted audit. The testing process and preparation of the external documentation give the developer the opportunity to review the entire application. Testing and preparation of much of the necessary external documentation can generally be accomplished at the same time. The results of testing will provide a major portion of the external documentation of the template.

TESTING

The testing examples presented in this chapter will not include macros. If macros are used in an application, testing would include the macros and macro control operations. Some users prefer testing an application twice, once without macros and again after macro menus have been added. This two-level approach allows the user to isolate macro testing as a second stage.

Testing a template or spreadsheet application is performed for two primary reasons. First, the accuracy of the template must be verified. Second, testing with the full range of possible values for all input items will ensure that the model can function for the full range of possible data environments.

Accuracy testing is the easiest testing task. The testing procedure should utilize several sets of possible input data. The first set of input data values should be selected so that they are easily verified through mental calculation or by using a calculator. Often, this set of data can be used in the initial design of the template as formulas and other outputs are developed. This first test set should detect any gross errors in formulas or cell references.

Following the successful test of the first set of test data, several additional sets of input data should be developed. The test data sets need to include a full range of possible values for each data item. This type of testing is extremely useful in detecting any limitations in the capacity of the template. Frequently a template will work well for the data set that the user had in mind at the time of the original design, but will fail when applied to more varied data sets.

Independent verification of output results is an important phase of the testing process. Otherwise, it can be quite easy for the user to repeatedly pass over the same error and miss the benefits of the testing process. Often, a problem set from a textbook that is known to be correct or a data set with correct results developed by another means can be used as a source for independent verification. In any case, some means of independent verification must be applied to all outputs generated in the worksheet.

Some of the problems or errors that can be detected through testing are:

- incorrect entry of a formula; errors in the formula or incorrect cell references
- incorrect range assignments
- column widths too small, or too large, to display the output correctly or conveniently
- incorrect output results for input values outside of the expected range of values
- template capacity limitations such as missing value entries in a lookup table or not all conditions handled in an @IF statement
- incorrect output results for input values outside of the "obvious" range of values

PAYROLL EXAMPLE, WITH TEST DATA

The payroll example will be used to illustrate the testing process. Be aware that this example is somewhat simplified for the purposes of convenience in presentation. An actual payroll application and the accompanying testing process will be somewhat more complex. The payroll example selected here does allow a demonstration of formula checking and a test of a lookup function.

The first set of test input data is presented in Figure 6-1.

A	A	B	C	D	E	F	G
33		INPUT AREA					|
34	Employee	Marital	Number of	Regular	Overtime	Hourly	|
35	Name	Status	Exemption	Hours	Hours	Wage	|
36	Earl Baker	S	0	80	0	$12.00	|
37	Carl Jones	S	1	80	0	$15.00	|
38	Jane Hamilton	S	2	80	0	$8.75	|
39	Peter Smith	S	3	80	0	$12.50	|
40	Angell Labourx	S	4	80	0	$8.90	|
41	Esther Albertson	S	5	80	0	$6.25	|
42	Carrie Walker	M	0	80	0	$13.00	|
43	James Brown	M	1	80	0	$12.00	|
44	Joan Caulfield	M	2	80	0	$8.50	|
45	Harvey Korman	M	3	80	0	$4.25	|
46	Jane Williams	M	4	80	0	$3.50	|
47	Peter Brown	M	5	80	0	$9.58	|
48							

A	H	I	J	K	L	M	N
33			OUTPUT AREA				
34	Regular	Overtime	Gross	Soc Sec	Federal	State	Net
35	Pay	Pay	Pay	FICA	FIT	SIT	Pay
36	$960.00	$0.00	$960.00	$72.10	$118.00	$48.00	$721.90
37	$1,200.00	$0.00	$1,200.00	$90.12	$103.00	$60.00	$946.88
38	$700.00	$0.00	$700.00	$52.57	$76.00	$35.00	$536.43
39	$1,000.00	$0.00	$1,000.00	$75.10	$78.00	$50.00	$796.90
40	$712.00	$0.00	$712.00	$53.47	$51.00	$35.60	$571.93
41	$500.00	$0.00	$500.00	$37.55	$9.00	$25.00	$428.45
42	$1,040.00	$0.00	$1,040.00	$78.10	$102.00	$52.00	$807.90
43	$960.00	$0.00	$960.00	$72.10	$90.00	$48.00	$749.90
44	$680.00	$0.00	$680.00	$51.07	$60.00	$34.00	$534.93
45	$340.00	$0.00	$340.00	$25.53	ERR	$17.00	ERR
46	$280.00	$0.00	$280.00	$21.03	ERR	$14.00	ERR
47	$766.40	$0.00	$766.40	$57.56	$36.00	$38.32	$634.52
48							

Figure 6-1 Payroll—Test Data Set 1—Input and Output Data

This first set of test data contains a value set that will be easy to use in checking output results with a calculator. In addition, a sample of possible data values is provided in the test set. The values used for number of exemptions ranges from 0 to 5. Marital status codes of both "M" and "S" are included. Hourly wage rates range from $15.00 to $3.50. And, all overtime hours are set to zero. In the second test set, overtime hour values will be included.

As can be seen in the output area, an error (marked by ERR) has occurred in the federal withholding tax computation. The formula for calculating the federal tax (FIT) involves use of a lookup function and use of two tables—one table for MARRIED withholdings and another for SINGLE withholdings. The tables are range-named MARRIED and SINGLE. The formula, as given for the first employee, is

```
@IF(+B36="S",@VLOOKUP(J36,$SINGLE,C36+1),
@VLOOKUP(J36,$MARRIED,C36+1))
```

Since the formula only involves the simple @IF, which appears to be working, the @VLOOKUP must be the incorrect component.

Both the married and single lookup tables are currently set up for salary ranges from $500–$800. The two employees generating the ERR result in the FIT column have gross pay of less than $500. There is no valid matching table entry for those two employees.

The format for the @VLOOKUP function is

```
@VLOOKUP(value to find, table location,
matching offset column)
```

An easy way to test a lookup function is to set the matching offset column to zero. In the payroll example the matching offset column is set to equal the number of exemptions plus 1. So, setting the offset value to zero will cause the lookup to return the matching salary entry (first column of the table) instead of the actual deduction. Using this technique, we can determine exactly which row of the table is being accessed by the lookup function. After setting the offset value to zero, the FIT formula appears as

```
@IF(+B36="S",@VLOOKUP(J36,$SINGLE,0),
@VLOOKUP(J36,$MARRIED,0))
```

This formula is used in the FIT calculation in the version in Figure 6-2.

A	H	I	J	K	L	M	N
33			OUTPUT AREA				
34	Regular	Overtime	Gross	Soc Sec	Federal	State	Net
35	Pay	Pay	Pay	FICA	FIT	SIT	Pay
36	$960.00	$0.00	$960.00	$72.10	$800.00	$48.00	$39.90
37	$1,200.00	$0.00	$1,200.00	$90.12	$800.00	$60.00	$249.88
38	$700.00	$0.00	$700.00	$52.57	$700.00	$35.00	($87.57)
39	$1,000.00	$0.00	$1,000.00	$75.10	$800.00	$50.00	$74.90
40	$712.00	$0.00	$712.00	$53.47	$700.00	$35.60	($77.07)
41	$500.00	$0.00	$500.00	$37.55	$500.00	$25.00	($62.55)
42	$1,040.00	$0.00	$1,040.00	$78.10	$800.00	$52.00	$109.90
43	$960.00	$0.00	$960.00	$72.10	$800.00	$48.00	$39.90
44	$680.00	$0.00	$680.00	$51.07	$680.00	$34.00	($85.07)
45	$340.00	$0.00	$340.00	$25.53	ERR	$17.00	ERR
46	$280.00	$0.00	$280.00	$21.03	ERR	$14.00	ERR
47	$766.40	$0.00	$766.40	$57.56	$760.00	$38.32	($89.48)
48							
49							
50							

Figure 6-2 Lookup Function Modified to Offset = Zero

It is evident in viewing the output that the lookup function is failing to locate a matching entry in the table. To correct this error, the lookup tables need to be modified. This modification will be accomplished by inserting two rows at the top of each table. The corrected tables are shown in Figure 6-3.

A	F	G	H	I	J	K	L	M	N
1		WORK AREA							
2									
3	MARRIED - Semimonthly payroll								
4	wages	allowances							
5		0	1	2	3	4	5	6	
6	0	$0	$0	$0	$0	$0	$0	$0	
7	250	$50	$42	$34	$26	$18	$10	$2	
8	$500	$57	$45	$33	$21	$9	$0	$0	
9	$520	$60	$48	$36	$24	$12	$0	$0	
10	$540	$63	$51	$39	$27	$15	$3	$0	
11	$560	$66	$54	$42	$30	$18	$6	$3	
12	$580	$69	$57	$45	$33	$21	$9	$6	
13	$600	$72	$60	$48	$36	$24	$12	$9	
14	$620	$75	$63	$51	$39	$27	$15	$12	
15	$640	$78	$66	$54	$42	$30	$18	$15	
16	$660	$81	$69	$57	$45	$33	$21	$18	
17	$680	$84	$72	$60	$48	$36	$24	$21	
18	$700	$87	$75	$63	$51	$39	$27	$24	
19	$720	$90	$78	$66	$54	$42	$30	$27	
20	$740	$93	$81	$69	$57	$45	$33	$30	
21	$760	$96	$84	$72	$60	$48	$36	$33	
22	$780	$99	$87	$75	$63	$51	$39	$36	
23	$800	$102	$90	$78	$66	$54	$42	$39	
24									

Figure 6-3A Lookup Table Modification

A	O	P	Q	R	S	T	U	V
1								
2								
3	SINGLE - Semimonthly payroll							
4	wages	allowances						
5		0	1	2	3	4	5	6
6	$0	$0	$0	$0	$0	$0	$0	$0
7	$250	$50	$38	$26	$14	$2	$0	$0
8	$500	$70	$58	$46	$33	$21	$9	$6
9	$520	$73	$61	$49	$36	$24	$12	$9
10	$540	$76	$64	$52	$39	$27	$15	$12
11	$560	$79	$67	$55	$42	$30	$18	$15
12	$580	$82	$70	$58	$45	$33	$21	$18
13	$600	$85	$73	$61	$48	$36	$24	$21
14	$620	$88	$76	$64	$51	$39	$27	$24
15	$640	$91	$79	$67	$54	$42	$30	$27
16	$660	$94	$82	$70	$57	$45	$33	$30
17	$680	$97	$85	$73	$60	$48	$36	$33
18	$700	$100	$88	$76	$63	$51	$39	$36
19	$720	$103	$91	$79	$66	$54	$42	$39
20	$740	$106	$94	$82	$69	$57	$45	$42
21	$760	$109	$97	$85	$72	$60	$48	$45
22	$780	$112	$100	$88	$75	$63	$51	$48
23	$800	$118	$103	$91	$78	$66	$54	$51
24								

Figure 6-3B Lookup Table Modification

The two additional entries in the table ensure that all values for gross pay from zero to $800 will find a matching entry. The number of deductions was also increased to accommodate a larger range of values for exemptions—zero to six. After the additions are made to each table, it is necessary to use / Range Name Create to redefine the ranges of the two tables. No change is required in the output formulas.

A second run of the test data in set 1 is shown in Figure 6-4.

A	H	I	J	K	L	M	N	O
35			OUTPUT AREA					
36	Regular	Overtime	Gross	Soc Sec	Federal	State		Net
37	Pay	Pay	Pay	FICA	FIT	SIT		Pay
38	$960.00	$0.00	$960.00	$72.10	$800.00	$48.00		$39.90
39	$1,200.00	$0.00	$1,200.00	$90.12	$800.00	$60.00		$249.88
40	$700.00	$0.00	$700.00	$52.57	$700.00	$35.00		($87.57)
41	$1,000.00	$0.00	$1,000.00	$75.10	$800.00	$50.00		$74.90
42	$712.00	$0.00	$712.00	$53.47	$700.00	$35.60		($77.07)
43	$500.00	$0.00	$500.00	$37.55	$500.00	$25.00		($62.55)
44	$1,040.00	$0.00	$1,040.00	$78.10	$800.00	$52.00		$109.90
45	$960.00	$0.00	$960.00	$72.10	$800.00	$48.00		$39.90
46	$680.00	$0.00	$680.00	$51.07	$680.00	$34.00		($85.07)
47	$340.00	$0.00	$340.00	$25.53	$250.00	$17.00		$47.47
48	$280.00	$0.00	$280.00	$21.03	$250.00	$14.00		($5.03)
49	$766.40	$0.00	$766.40	$57.56	$760.00	$38.32		($89.48)
50								

Figure 6-4 Payroll—Rerun of Test Data Set 1—Offset = Zero

The offset value is still set to zero in the FIT lookup formula, and the results displayed in the FIT column indicate that a successful match has been found for each gross pay value. Note that the net pay column is incorrect because of its reference to the FIT column. After the offset value is returned to its correct setting, the net pay formula can be verified.

The final and correct results of the payroll run of test data set 1 is shown in Figure 6-5. Now that the lookup is functioning, a calculator will be needed to test each of the other output column formulas.

A	A	B	C	D	E	F
35		INPUT AREA				
36	Employee	Marital	Number of	Regular	Overtime	Hourly
37	Name	Status	Exemption	Hours	Hours	Wage
38	Earl Baker	S	0	80	0	$12.00
39	Carl Jones	S	1	80	0	$15.00
40	Jane Hamilton	S	2	80	0	$8.75
41	Peter Smith	S	3	80	0	$12.50
42	Angell Labourx	S	4	80	0	$8.90
43	Esther Albertson	S	5	80	0	$6.25
44	Carrie Walker	M	0	80	0	$13.00
45	James Brown	M	1	80	0	$12.00
46	Joan Caulfield	M	2	80	0	$8.50
47	Harvey Korman	M	3	80	0	$4.25
48	Jane Williams	M	4	80	0	$3.50
49	Peter Brown	M	5	80	0	$9.58
50						
51						

A	H	I	J	K	L	M	N	O
35			OUTPUT AREA					
36	Regular	Overtime	Gross	Soc Sec	Federal	State		Net
37	Pay	Pay	Pay	FICA	FIT	SIT		Pay
38	$960.00	$0.00	$960.00	$72.10	$118.00	$48.00		$721.90
39	$1,200.00	$0.00	$1,200.00	$90.12	$103.00	$60.00		$946.88
40	$700.00	$0.00	$700.00	$52.57	$76.00	$35.00		$536.43
41	$1,000.00	$0.00	$1,000.00	$75.10	$78.00	$50.00		$796.90
42	$712.00	$0.00	$712.00	$53.47	$51.00	$35.60		$571.93
43	$500.00	$0.00	$500.00	$37.55	$9.00	$25.00		$428.45
44	$1,040.00	$0.00	$1,040.00	$78.10	$102.00	$52.00		$807.90
45	$960.00	$0.00	$960.00	$72.10	$90.00	$48.00		$749.90
46	$680.00	$0.00	$680.00	$51.07	$60.00	$34.00		$534.93
47	$340.00	$0.00	$340.00	$25.53	$26.00	$17.00		$271.47
48	$280.00	$0.00	$280.00	$21.03	$18.00	$14.00		$226.97
49	$766.40	$0.00	$766.40	$57.56	$36.00	$38.32		$634.52
50								
51								

Figure 6-5 Payroll—Final Run, Test Data Set 1—Input and Output Data

Following the successful test of data set 1, a second set of test data is entered and output results are again checked. Remember, we have not tested the overtime calculation in the first data set. The second test data includes a typical range of values for overtime. This test is immediately successful, as shown in Figure 6-6.

For most applications, several sets of test data should be used to determine that all possible conditions have been handled correctly in the worksheet.

FORMULA ERRORS

There is one formula error that is especially troublesome and difficult to correct. If the letters "CIRC" appear at the bottom of the screen, there is a circular calculation error in the spreadsheet. If this condition occurs, there are one or more formulas that have a reference to themselves. To locate a cell that contains the circular reference, use the command series / Worksheet Status (in Lotus). This command will display the cell address of the cell containing a circular reference. Refer to this cell address and correct the formula. If the "CIRC" indicator still displays, there are more cells with this troublesome error. Use the / Worksheet Status command again to find the next CIRC cell address. Continue this process until the CIRC indicator is gone. Some overall review of all formulas should follow a CIRC error. With good design, such an error should not occur. Usually not all input data and constants have been identified and separately located in the input area. Some redesign may be required to fully correct the CIRC error properly.

A	A	B	C	D	E	F	G
35		INPUT AREA					|
36	Employee	Marital	Number of	Regular	Overtime	Hourly	|
37	Name	Status	Exemption	Hours	Hours	Wage	|
38	Earl Baker	S	0	75	0	$12.00	|
39	Carl Jones	S	1	80	5	$15.00	|
40	Jane Hamilton	S	2	80	6	$8.75	|
41	Peter Smith	S	3	80	10	$12.50	|
42	Angell Labourx	S	4	80	2	$8.90	|
43	Esther Albertson	S	5	80	0	$6.25	|
44	Carrie Walker	M	0	80	9	$13.00	|
45	James Brown	M	1	80	4	$12.00	|
46	Joan Caulfield	M	2	80	6	$8.50	|
47	Harvey Korman	M	3	80	15	$4.25	|
48	Jane Williams	M	4	80	0	$3.50	|
49	Peter Brown	M	5	80	5	$9.58	|
50							

A	H	I	J	K	L	M	N	O
35			OUTPUT AREA					
36	Regular	Overtime	Gross	Soc Sec	Federal	State		Net
37	Pay	Pay	Pay	FICA	FIT	SIT		Pay
38	$900.00	$0.00	$900.00	$67.59	$118.00	$45.00		$669.41
39	$1,200.00	$112.50	$1,312.50	$98.57	$103.00	$65.63		$1,045.30
40	$700.00	$78.75	$778.75	$58.48	$85.00	$38.94		$596.33
41	$1,000.00	$187.50	$1,187.50	$89.18	$78.00	$59.38		$960.94
42	$712.00	$26.70	$738.70	$55.48	$54.00	$36.94		$592.28
43	$500.00	$0.00	$500.00	$37.55	$9.00	$25.00		$428.45
44	$1,040.00	$175.50	$1,215.50	$91.28	$102.00	$60.78		$961.44
45	$960.00	$72.00	$1,032.00	$77.50	$90.00	$51.60		$812.90
46	$680.00	$76.50	$756.50	$56.81	$69.00	$37.83		$592.86
47	$340.00	$95.63	$435.63	$32.72	$26.00	$21.78		$355.13
48	$280.00	$0.00	$280.00	$21.03	$18.00	$14.00		$226.97
49	$766.40	$71.85	$838.25	$62.95	$42.00	$41.91		$691.39
50								

Figure 6-6 Payroll—Test Data Set 2—Input and Output Data

EXTERNAL DOCUMENTATION

External documentation can be easily developed as a byproduct of the testing process. The printed results of each set of test data should be documented by printing the entire resulting worksheet in the As-Displayed format. If the test data is complete and well chosen, this documentation presents a description of the full range of values that can be used in the template. A listing of the template formulas printed in the Cell-Formulas format should also be included in the external documentation. The Cell-Formulas format is a better choice than reformatting cells in TEXT mode for this documentation. The Cell-Formulas format will always print the entire formula and does not require adjustment of column widths for long formulas. The practice of widening columns to display a TEXT mode formula is tedious and can result in making the worksheet hard to read as a whole. If all columns are not sufficiently widened, a portion of the formula may be truncated.

The printing of the dated input/output test results of the template provides a useful internal control. The test results and the actual testing process is documented in physical form for internal audit and control purposes. Note that printed reports are superior to computer-readable media for some control purposes since dates and other information are easily modifiable on computer-readable media.

Along with the printed test results, worksheet files stored on a computer-readable medium should be saved and maintained. These test data worksheets can be useful whenever template modifications are needed. The modifications can be made on one of the test worksheets and immediately tested with that set of test data. The other sets of test data can also be easily applied to the modified template. This practice provides real efficiencies and helps ensure that testing is applied to the modified template as thoroughly as it was applied to the original version.

To summarize, external documentation should include the following items:

1. a master copy of the spreadsheet saved to a single diskette (one application per disk)
2. a one-to-three page explanation of the application—its purpose, who will be using it, and how it will be used
3. a printed copy of results of each test data set (include a version with each test data set saved to a separate file, on diskette, for ease in testing or running an audit at a later date)
4. a printed copy of the entire worksheet, in As-Displayed format
5. a printed copy of the entire worksheet, in Cell-Formulas format
6. a sample of each designed output—to include graphs, simple reports, and reports using special forms (include a copy of the graph settings screen and print settings screen with the sample outputs)
7. an explanation and listing of all internal controls used in the application, including all uses of hash totals, batch totals, and data edit checks
8. a chronological listing of modifications (assuming the current documentation is of the most recent version)

If complex macros are used, some additional explanation of their operation may be added to the above documentation.

LAYOUT AND DESIGN EXERCISES

1. Develop three sets of test data suitable for testing the 3-year pro forma income projection presented in Figure 3-2. Be sure to select test data that checks the limits of the model as well as the expected normal operation.
2. Develop a complete set of external documentation for the 3-year pro forma income projection model (Figure 3-2). Which of the items included in the documentation are most useful?
3. Develop a set of test data, perform the tests, and develop a complete set of external documentation for the checkbook register, Figure 3-3.
4. What kind of testing would you use on the customer address file, Figure 3-7?

Chapter 7 MACRO DESIGN

Designing macros is usually the last step in the design of an application. Effective use of macros completes the design of an application and can add a level of organization and control to the entire application. Spreadsheet macros can greatly enhance the capabilities and appearance of spreadsheet applications. A simple macro can be built to replace a long, tedious series of keystrokes. More complex macros can be used to provide customized menus that can control all aspects of the application, from data entry to display of graphs and printing.

For good spreadsheet design, the challenge is to use macros in a useful and effective way. A few guidelines for such appropriate use are provided.

1. Use macros to automate tasks that will be repeatedly required in the application. These include such tasks as
   - printing standard areas or ranges of the spreadsheet
   - generating graphs with the same definition parameters
   - controlling data entry
   - clearing a template to zeroes

2. Use range names whenever possible in macros. The same benefits of additional clarity and ease in making modifications are gained with the use of range names in macros as by using them in formulas.
3. Do NOT use macros to perform calculations that can be accomplished with standard formulas or functions. Standard formulas and functions are more immediately understandable, efficient, and accurate than user-built macros. The spreadsheet software developers have already designed several error-detection/prevention features to work with cell formulas. User-built macros may be more prone to error and may require more testing to ensure accuracy.
4. Whenever possible, use macro menus to organize and document the macros available for a given worksheet or application. Generating a set of single-key macro commands to replace long series of keystrokes can be a great convenience to a single user. But what if another user wishes to work with the same application? Putting keystroke macros into macro menus allows the user easy access of these menus when needed and provides a useful method of internally documenting the macro set.
5. If a macro menu is used, define the menu with the name \0 or \M. Then the menu will either start automatically when the spreadsheet file is retrieved, or can be called with the ALT M command. Using a standard name for all menus makes menu access convenient for all users.
6. Be careful to use range names that are not identical to advanced macro commands or to cursor movement controls such as RIGHT, LEFT, UP, DOWN, and HOME. If you should assign a keyword as one of your defined range names, your range name will take precedence and the Lotus command will be disabled.

A discussion of complex macro design is beyond the scope of this book. However, a few illustrations of how macros can be utilized will be shown. We will use some of the spreadsheet examples presented in earlier chapters.

MACROS FOR MONTHLY BUDGET PROJECTION—MACRO MENU

A simple macro menu has been created for the monthly budget projection example in Figure 7-1.

```
A   O        P                                              Q                     R                     S
4   MACRO AREA
5
6   \M       {MENUBRANCH MENU1}
7
8   MENU1    INPUT                                          PRINT                 SAVE                  EXIT
9            Input new data                                 Print budget report   Save current file     Exit from menu
10           {GOTO}CHGRATE~                                 /PPRreport~AGQ        /FS{?}~               {QUIT}
11           {GETNUMBER "Enter expected change rate:",chgrate} {MENUBRANCH MENU1} {MENUBRANCH MENU1}
12           {DOWN 3}
13           {GETNUMBER "Enter wages:",wages}
14           {DOWN 3}
15           {GETNUMBER "Enter rent:",rent}
16           {DOWN}
17           {GETNUMBER "Enter car payment:",carpyt}
18           {DOWN}
19           {GETNUMBER "Enter child care costs:",childcare}
20           {DOWN}
21           {GETNUMBER "Enter utilities:",util}
22           {DOWN}
23           {GETNUMBER "Enter household expenses:",house}
24           {DOWN}
25           {GETNUMBER "Enter miscellaneous expenses:",misc}
26           {CALC}
27           {MENUBRANCH MENU1}
28
29
```

Figure 7-1 Monthly Budget Projection—Simple Macro Menu

This macro has a typical set of options that control the basic operational tasks for this application. Data entry, printing, file save, and a menu exit are supplied. Most macro menus will have a similar set of choices controlling input, output, and data storage.

A macro menu such as this is actually like a program. A basic rule of programming is that each module has one entry point and one exit point. That is the purpose behind the MENUBRANCH command at the end of every menu option except the last EXIT option. Control always should return to the top level of the menu and exit from the menu at that level.

MACRO LIBRARY MENU

Many spreadsheet users get "macro-happy" and create a large set of convenience macros that are generally used to replace time-consuming and routine keystroke series. Changing column-widths, formatting cell ranges, setting printer controls, and inserting date and time into a cell are examples of some of the routines that are often replaced by macros. The problem with creating a large number of these keystroke macros is that they can be as difficult to remember as the keystroke series was tedious. If another user works with the application, that person may have an even more difficult time utilizing the macro library.

The most effective way to organize such a library is to arrange all of the commands in a cascading menu. An example is provided in Figure 7-2.

A	V	W	X	Y	Z	AA	AB
4	MACRO LIBRARY						
5							
6	\L	{MENUBRANCH LIBRARY}					
7							
8	LIBRARY	Column-widths	Formats	Date-stamp	Exit		
9		Change column widths	Select range formats	Enter current date	Exit from menu		
10		{MENUBRANCH WIDTHS}	{MENUBRANCH FORMATS}	{MENUBRANCH DATES}	{QUIT}		
11							
12	WIDTHS	Set-to-20	Select-width	Exit			
13		Set current column to 20	Enter width from keyboard	Return to LIBRARY menu			
14		/wcs20~	/wcs{?}~	{MENUBRANCH LIBRARY}			
15		{MENUBRANCH LIBRARY}	{MENUBRANCH LIBRARY}				
16							
17	FORMATS	Currency	Percent	Exit			
18		Currency-2 decimal places	Percent - 0 places	Return to LIBRARY menu}			
19		/rfc~~	/rfp0~	{MENUBRANCH LIBRARY}			
20		{MENUBRANCH LIBRARY}	{MENUBRANCH LIBRARY}				
21							
22	DATES	Today	Tomorrow	Time	Exit		
23		Enter today's date	Enter tomorrow's date	Enter time	Return to LIBRARY menu		
24		@TODAY~	@TODAY-1~	@NOW~	{MENUBRANCH LIBRARY}		
25		/rfd1~	/rfd1~	/rfdt2~			
26		{MENUBRANCH LIBRARY}	{MENUBRANCH LIBRARY}	{MENUBRANCH LIBRARY}			
27							
28							

Figure 7-2 Macro Library—Menu Format

This macro library can be used in two different ways. The macro library menu can be accessed using the ALT L command. The user drops through the menu levels to the desired choice. To make this method effective, the menu headings have to organize the tasks in a top-down or hierarchical structure. Such a top-down organization is illustrated in this example. The "Column-widths" option at the top level drops down to the "Widths" option at the next level. The "Widths" level provides an array of choices, one of which is selected for execution. The "Widths" level exits by returning to the top level. If further menu levels are desired, a {MENUBRANCH. . .} can access the next level. Again, the entire menu has one exit point at the EXIT option of the top level.

Care should be taken that these macro library menus remain reasonable in size and complexity. Options can be selected so that only the most commonly used choices are totally automated. One option can always be designed to allow input from the keyboard. In the "WIDTHS" level of the menu, one option is designed to automatically set a column-width to size 20. A second option is designed to allow the user to enter the preferred width from the keyboard.

The second way the macro library can be used is by assigning individual macro names to each of the keystroke series located in the library. Then, if a user does not wish to use the library menu, the single-letter macro command can be used. Each macro in such a library will be able to be executed through the cascading menu or by using the single-letter name (ALT + letter-name).

LAYOUT AND DESIGN EXERCISES

1. Develop a macro menu for the 3-year income projection (Figure 3-2) and the accompanying graphs (Figure 5-3 for a pie chart and Figure 5-4 for a stacked-bar graph). Set up menu options to control data entry, to view both the pie chart and bar graph after a new set of input data has been entered, and to save the current file under a file name supplied by the user via the keyboard.
2. Create a small macro library menu that includes a series of options for setting up printer controls. Create an option that defines settings for condensed print, regular-size print, and a 6-line mailing label.

Chapter 8 AUDIT AND DESIGN REVIEW

As a final review of design issues and considerations for spreadsheet applications, it will be useful to examine the process and requirements of an internal audit as applied to spreadsheets. The audit of a spreadsheet application is performed to verify compliance with several aspects of operation and control. If the business has established a set of design guidelines for spreadsheet applications, a compliance audit would be conducted to ensure that these guidelines have been followed. For spreadsheet applications that involve the basic financial transactions of the business, there will need to be a set of specific internal controls to verify the correctness of the information and help prevent or detect error and fraud. Such controls should definitely be established for any spreadsheet-based accounting, payroll, and inventory applications.

Applications such as these would be subjected to some level of review or audit. The purpose of the audit in this case is to determine whether the prescribed operational controls are being followed and are sufficient.

A full treatment of spreadsheet auditing is beyond the scope of this book. However, spreadsheet designers need to be aware of auditing concerns when building their applications. Not every template will be subjected to an actual internal or external audit. However, many of the concerns raised by the prospect of meeting an audit are the same as those raised by spreadsheet design standards.

Controls will be required for both the development stage and the operational stage. The types of internal controls required in the development stage involve

- layout and documentation standards
- testing: both data testing and validity testing
- modification procedures: testing and documentation

The types of internal controls required in the operational stage involve

- management of processing: data entry, report generation, and backup procedures
- accuracy and reliability of processing: maintaining control totals, reconciliations, output review
- management of personnel functions: areas of responsibility, supervision, and security
- management of physical security: access, storage, and protective controls

The main purpose of this chapter is to identify and present a general set of guidelines or internal controls suitable for the development stage. These guidelines can be further developed and specified by the business or organization into a set of spreadsheet standards suitable for the specific uses and applications of that business.

The introduction of the concerns involved in the operational audit are also pertinent to the spreadsheet designer. Some of the operational controls require implementation within the worksheet itself. Accuracy controls such as hash totals and reconciliations are obvious examples.

The concept of control, as applied to spreadsheet design, seems to meet a certain resistance. Many microcomputer environments have been sorely lacking in adequate controls. The flexibility and freedom typically shown by employees working with desktop or laptop computers have been a source of both creativity and chaos for their businesses or organizations. Because the microcomputer marketing strategy has focused so strongly on the individual user, emphasis on standards and controls has been minimal. Yet, when management reviews the kind of decision-making that depends on spreadsheets, the benefits of some kind of control should be apparent.

OPERATIONAL CONTROLS—PAYROLL APPLICATION

We will use the payroll example again to present a typical set of operational controls. Each of the operational areas will be addressed. These areas include physical security and backup, processing management, and personnel controls.

PHYSICAL CONTROLS AND SECURITY—DAILY LOG

Every use of the payroll application should be recorded in a daily log. The log would contain entries under such headings as DATE OF USE, USER'S NAME, TYPE OF ACTIVITY (update or report), BACKUP DISK NUMBER. The log would be monitored and approved by the immediate supervisor on a regular basis. The "logbook" approach is useful in that it identifies standard procedures, records the completion of those procedures, and identifies the person responsible for completing the procedures.

One of the standard procedures recorded in the logbook is backup. Frequent backups are the best insurance against data loss or destruction. One or more backups should be made after EVERY data entry session. Surprisingly, the lack of regular backups is the major cause of data loss. Lack of a current, valid backup occurs much more frequently than fire, flood, or earthquake. At least two or three backup copies should be kept on the work site. Periodic cumulative backups should be stored at an off-site premise. Storage of all backup copies of financial data should be kept in a disaster-proof container. The best approach to backup is to plan for it as a standard activity that accompanies the data entry process.

Several other physical controls will be commonly applied to all data processing activities at any business or organization. Such controls are usually the responsibility of computer services management rather than the individual spreadsheet designer.

PROCESSING MANAGEMENT—CONTROLS CHECKLIST

The hash totals, cross-checks, batch totals, and data edit checks so carefully designed into the spreadsheet application reap their benefits at the operational stage. In the payroll application, hash totals for the ID or Social Security numbers can be checked against past and future totals. Batch totals and cross-checks can be verified. The data edit checks for reasonable values for hours worked, wage rates, and final net pay will have prevented some data entry errors.

Each of the controls that were designed for the application should be reviewed and the results of the control verified. Often, a checklist is used for every run or use of the model. The checklist documents the controls and instructs the user in the method of verifying the results. The checklist will be filled out and signed by all responsible persons. This checklist is stored and used to audit or review the process whenever necessary.

PERSONNEL CONTROLS

A basic rule of personnel control in the operation of any critical data processing system is: NEVER ALLOW ONE PERSON FULL RESPONSIBILITY FOR AN ENTIRE SYSTEM! This rule should be applied to critical processing activities using spreadsheets as well as to mainframe activities. As applied to the payroll application, the following controls could be established:

- The person who receives and records time cards (normally the payroll clerk) does not hand out the payroll checks.
- The payroll check register is printed by someone other than the payroll clerk. Control totals on the payroll register report are verified by someone other than the payroll clerk. (The controls checklist is to be signed and finalized by all responsible persons—generally more than one person.)
- All payroll check forms are accounted for, whether they are pre-numbered or not. All void forms are documented and disposed of in a secure way.

Not all of the operational controls are the responsibility of the spreadsheet designer, but awareness of these requirements is useful in ensuring a design that can function within the expected operational environment.

SPREADSHEET AUDIT CHECKLIST

More important to the focus of this chapter are the controls applied to the development of the spreadsheet application. The need for proper layout, documentation, and testing have been addressed in detail in the previous chapters. As a final tool that can be useful for spreadsheet designers, a detailed checklist is provided here. The checklist could be used by the original designer in a final review process. The internal audit department could also use the checklist as a tool for a standards or compliance audit.

FINAL PERSPECTIVE

There are people, including managers, who ascribe a touch of infallibility to spreadsheet models and computer printouts. This can happen to people who are computer "techies" as well as to people who are somewhat intimidated by computers. The microcomputer and its array of software tools, including spreadsheets, can create a false sense of control or security. There are people who deplore the current approach to management with its focus on the quantitative aspects and yearn for the good old days when good judgment equaled good decision-making. Are all of these computer-based tools helping managers to generate better decisions? Are our computer-based tools helping us to think better, both analytically and creatively? If we are thinking better, the tools are serving their purpose. Technology should serve, not overwhelm. The spreadsheet users who apply the principles of proper design, documentation, and testing to their spreadsheet applications will have found an excellent support for good thinking.

SPREADSHEET AUDIT CHECKLIST **Date of audit** ______________________

PERSON CONDUCTING THE AUDIT ______________________

TITLE OF WORKSHEET ______________________

WORKSHEET AUTHOR ______________________

LAYOUT and INTERNAL DOCUMENTATION:

Input variables defined and separated from output **YES** ___ **NO**___

Regions included in worksheet: (check if present)

IDENTIFICATION AREA ___

CONTROL AREA ___

DEFINITIONS, ASSUMPTIONS, and FORMULAS ___

RANGE NAME TABLE ___

GRAPHS TABLE ___

WORK AREA ___

LAYOUT MAP ___

INPUT DATA IN DATABASE FORMAT ___

Comments: ______________________

____

OUTPUT AREAS: (check if present)

OUTPUT AREA FOR DATA, CALCULATED RESULTS ___

OUTPUT AREA FOR SPECIAL REPORT FORMATS ___

ATTACHED GRAPHS ___

Comments: ______________________

____

MACROS: (check if present)

MENU FORMAT **YES** ___ **NO** ___

automatic \0 **YES** ___ **NO** ___

\M **YES** ___ **NO** ___

\L for macro library **YES** ___ **NO** ___

Other macros **YES** ___ **NO** ___

Comments: ______________________

____

TESTING:

Number of test data sets ______

Accurate results from all sets of test data YES ___ NO ___

Comments: ____

____

EXTERNAL DOCUMENTATION FILE:

1. **Master copy on single diskette YES ___ NO ___**
2. **Explanation of application YES ___ NO ___**
3. **Printed copy of test data and results YES ___ NO ___**
4. **Printed copy of worksheet—AS-DISPLAYED YES ___ NO ___**
5. **Printed copy of worksheet—CELL-FORMULAS YES ___ NO ___**
6. **Sample of each output (with documentation) YES ___ NO ___**
7. **Internal controls listing YES ___ NO ___**

   Operational controls checklist YES ___ NO ___
8. **Chronology of modifications YES ___ NO ___**

Comments: ____

____

AUDIT ACCEPTANCE—AUTHORIZATION:

APPROVED: ____

NOT APPROVED: ____

REQUIRED CHANGES OR ADDITIONS: ______________________________

____

____

____

____

LAYOUT AND DESIGN EXERCISES

1. Perform a full audit, using the audit checklist at the end of this chapter, on the 3-year income projection application that you documented as an exercise in Chapter 7.
2. In what circumstances will it be feasible to use the Spreadsheet Audit Checklist?
3. Are there any changes you would make to the Spreadsheet Audit Checklist? State your rationale for each of these changes.
4. Develop a full set of operational controls for the customer address file, Figure 3-8. Is any separation of personnel responsibilities required for this application?

INDEX